WORLDLINK

Developing English Fluency

Level 3

Nancy Douglas

James R. Morgan

NATIONAL GEOGRAPHIC LEARNING

CENGAGE Learning·

Australia • Brazil • Mexico • Singapore • United Kingdom • United States

World Link Level 3: Developing English Fluency, Third Edition
Nancy Douglas, Author
James R. Morgan, Author
Susan Stempleski, Series Editor

Publisher: Sherrise Roehr

Executive Editor: Sarah Kenney

Senior Development Editor: Brenden Layte

Associate Development Editor: Alison Bruno

Assistant Editor: Patricia Giunta

Media Researcher: Leila Hishmeh

Senior Technology Product Manager:
   Lauren Krolick

Director of Global Marketing: Ian Martin

Senior Product Marketing Manager:
   Caitlin Thomas

Sr. Director, ELT & World Languages:
   Michael Burggren

Production Manager: Daisy Sosa

Content Project Manager: Beth Houston

Senior Print Buyer: Mary Beth Hennebury

Composition: Lumina

Cover/Text Design: Brenda Carmichael

Art Director: Brenda Carmichael

Cover Image: Reed Saxon/Associated Press

Inside Front Cover Image: AFP/Getty Images

Photo Credits are listed on the inside
   back cover.

For product information and technology assistance, contact us at
Cengage Learning Customer & Sales Support, 1-800-354-9706
For permission to use material from this text or product,
submit all requests online at **www.cengage.com/permissions**
Further permissions questions can be emailed to
permissionrequest@cengage.com

World Link 3 ISBN: 978-1-305-65120-3

World Link 3 + My World Link Online ISBN: 978-1-305-65121-0

National Geographic Learning
20 Channel Center Street
Boston, MA 02210
USA

Cengage Learning is a leading provider of customized learning solutions with employees residing in nearly 40 different countries and sales in more than 125 countries around the world. Find your local representative at **www.cengage.com**

Cengage Learning products are represented in Canada by Nelson Education, Ltd.

Visit National Geographic Learning online at ngl.cengage.com
Visit our corporate website at **cengage.com**

Printed in the United States of America
Print Number: 03   Print Year: 2016

Acknowledgments

We would like to extend a very special thank you to the Instituto Cultural Peruano Norteamericano (ICPNA) academic management staff in the central office, branches and teachers, for the helpful insights and suggestions that contributed toward the development of this series.

We would also like to thank Raúl Billini, Educational Consultant, Santo Domingo, Dominican Republic, for his contributions to this series.

Thank you to the educators who provided invaluable feedback throughout the development of the *World Link* series: Rocio Abarca, Instituto Tecnológico de Costa Rica / FUNDATEC; David Aduviri, CBA (Centro Boliviano Americano) - La Paz; Ramon Aguilar, Universidad Tecnológica de Hermosillo; Miguel Arrazola, CBA (Centro Boliviano Americano) - Santa Cruz; Cecilia Avila, Universidad de Xalapa; Isabel Baracat, CCI (Centro de Comunicação Inglesa); Daniel Sanchez Bedoy, Calfornia Language Center; Andrea Brotto, CEICOM (Centro de Idiomas para Comunidades); George Bozanich, Soongsil University; Emma Campo, Universidad Central; Andrea Carlson, Aichi Prefectural University; Martha Carrasco, Universidad Autonoma de Sinaloa; Herbert Chavel, Korea Advanced Institute of Science and Technology; J. Ventura Chavez, Universidad de Guadalajara CUSUR; Denise de Bartolomeo, AMICANA (Asociación Mendocina de Intercambio Cultural Argentino Norteamericano); Rodrigo de Campos Rezende, SEVEN Idiomas; John Dennis, Hokuriku University; Kirvin Andrew Dyer, Yan Ping High School; Marilena Fernandes, Alumni; Mark Firth, J.F. Oberlin University; Daniela Frillochi, ARICANA (Asociación Rosarina de Intercambio Cultural Argentino Norteamericano); Joseph Gabriella, Toyo University; Marina Gonzalez, Instituto Universitario de Lenguas Modernas; Robert Gordon, Korea Advanced Institute of Science and Technology; Scott Grigas, Youngsan University; Gu Yingruo, Research Institute of Xiangzhou District, ZhuHai; Kyle Hammel, Incheon National University; Mariana Gil Hammer, Instituto Cultural Dominico Americano; Helen Hanae, Toyo University; Xu Heng, Nantong Polytechnic College; Amiris Helena, Centro Cultural Dominico Americano; Rafael Hernandez, Centro Educacional Tlaquepaque; Yo-Tien Ho, Takming University; Marie Igwe, Hanseo University; Roxana Jimenez, Instituto Tecnológico de Costa Rica / FUNDATEC; Liu Jing, Shanghai Foreign Language Education Press; Lâm Nguyễn Huỳnh, Van Lang University; Hui-Chuan Liao, National Kaohsiung University of Applied Sciences; Pan Lang, Nanjing Sport Institute; Sirina Kainongsuang, Perfect Publishing Company Limited; Karen Ko, ChinYi University; Ching-Hua Lin, National Taiwan University of Science and Technology; Simon Liu, ChinYi University; Maria Helena Luna, Tronwell; Ady Marrero, Alianza Cultural Uruguay Estados Unidos; Nancy Mcaleer, ELC Universidad Interamericana de Panama; Michael McCallister, Feng Chia University Language Center; José Antonio Mendes Lopes, ICBEU (Instituto Cultural Brasil Estados Unidos); Tania Molina, Instituto Tecnológico de Costa Rica / FUNDATEC; Iliana Mora, Instituto Tecnológico de Costa Rica / FUNDATEC; Fernando Morales, Universidad Tecnológica de Hermosillo; Vivian Morghen, ICANA (Instituto Cultural Argentino Norteamericano); Aree Na Nan, Chiang Mai University; He Ning, Nanjing Mochou Vocational School; Paul Nugent, Kkottongnae University; Niu Yuchun, New Oriental School Beijing; Elizabeth Ortiz, COPEI (Copol English Institute); Virginia Ortiz, Universidad Autonoma de Tamaulipas; Marshall Presnick, Language Link Vietnam; Justin Prock, Pyeongtaek University; Peter Reilly, Universidad Bonaterra; Ren Huijun, New Oriental School Hangzhou; Andreina Romero, URBE (Universidad Rafael Belloso Chacín); Leon Rose, Jeonju University; Chris Ruddenklau, Kinki University; Adelina Ruiz, Instituto Tecnologico de Estudios Superiores de Occidente; Eleonora Salas, IICANA (Instituto de Intercambio Cultural Argentino Norteamericano); Jose Salas, Universidad Tecnológica del Norte de Guanajuato; Mary Sarawit, Naresuan University International College; Jenay Seymour, Hong-ik University; Huang Shuang, Shanghai International Studies University; Sávio Siqueira, ACBEU (Asociação Cultural Brasil Estados Unidos) / UFBA (Universidade Federal da Bahia); Beatriz Solina, ARICANA (Asociación Rosarina de Intercambio Cultural Argentino Norteamericano); Mari Cruz Suárez, Servicio de Idiomas UAM; Bambang Sujianto, Intensive English Course (IEC); Howard Tarnoff, Health Sciences University of Hokkaido; Emily J. Thomas, Incheon National University; Sandrine Ting, St. John's University; Tran Nguyen Hoai Chi, Vietnam USA Society English Training Service Center; Ruth Tun, Universidad Autonoma de Campeche; Rubén Ucela, Centro Cultural Dominico Americano; Maria Inés Valsecchi, Universidad Nacional de Río Cuarto; Alicia Vazquez, Instituto Internacional; Patricia Veciño, ICANA (Instituto Cultural Argentino Norteamericano); Punchalee Wasanasomsithi, Chulalongkorn University; Tomoe Watanabe, Hiroshima City University; Dhunyawat Treenate, Rajamangala University of Technology Krungthep; Haibo Wei, Nantong Agricultural College; Tomohiro Yanagi, Chubu University; Jia Yuan, Global IELTS School; Selestin Zainuddin, LBPP-LIA.

SCOPE & SEQUENCE

Grammar	Pronunciation	Speaking	Reading	Writing	Communication
Stative passive voice pp. 8, 193 Giving permission and expressing prohibition pp. 14, 194	Saying a series of items p. 6	Making informal suggestions p. 7	Creating public spaces p. 12 Make and check predictions Scan for information Infer information Read for details	Write about an annoying behavior p. 14	Describing and planning a presentation about how to fix a room p. 9 Talking about annoying behaviors p. 15
Review of future forms pp. 22, 195 Modals of future possibility pp. 28, 196	Content word emphasis p. 20	Talking about plans and needs p. 21	John Francis: The planet walker p. 26 Make predictions Infer meaning Scan for details	Write about your future plans p. 29	Predicting the future p. 23 Talking about future plans p. 29
Participial and prepositional phrases pp. 36, 197 Review of the present perfect pp. 42, 198	Stress: Verb + preposition p. 34	Interrupting someone politely p. 35	Viral news p. 40 Use background knowledge Sequence events Make connections Summarize	Share personal information p. 43	Ranking behaviors p. 37 Catching up at a reunion p. 43
Adverbs used with the present perfect pp. 54, 199 Phrasal verbs pp. 60, 200	Coarticulation p. 60	Disagreeing politely p. 53	Dating around the world p. 58 Use background knowledge Read for details Infer information	Continue a love story p. 60	Discussing social norms over time p. 55 Taking and discussing a dating survey p. 61
It + be + adjective + infinitive; Gerund + be + adjective pp. 68, 201 Present and future time clauses with before, after, when, as soon as / once pp. 74, 202	Linking the same sounds p. 66	Asking about culturally appropriate behavior p. 67	Welcome to Bogotá p. 72 Use background knowledge Understand purpose	Prepare a "how-to" presentation p. 75	Designing a poster to improve public behavior p. 69 Explaining how to do something p. 75
The passive voice: simple present and simple past pp. 82, 203 Connecting ideas with because, so, although / even though pp. 88, 204	Stress on nouns and verbs with the same spelling p. 80	Asking about companies / Emphasizing important points p. 81	Life without ads? p. 86 Identify a point of view Draw conclusions Scan for details	Write a product review p. 88	Presenting facts about your city or region p. 83 Creating a commercial p. 89

Grammar	Pronunciation	Speaking	Reading	Writing	Communication
Describing symptoms pp. 100, 206 Reported speech: commands and requests pp. 106, 207	The schwa sound p. 100	Giving, accepting, and refusing serious advice p. 99	Modern health problems p. 104 Scan for information Make predictions Check predictions Read for details Infer meaning	Write about a healthy change p. 106	Suggesting an alternative treatment p. 101 Giving tips for a healthy life p. 107
The present perfect vs. the present perfect continuous pp. 114, 208 Review: The simple past vs. the present perfect vs. the present perfect continuous pp. 120, 209	Stress in compound nouns p. 112	Explaining the set-up and rules of a game p. 113	A star in the X Games p. 118 Use background knowledge Scan for information Read for details	Write about a hobby p. 121	Talking about a new skill p. 115 Interviewing classmates about hobbies p. 121
Too and *enough* pp. 128, 210 Future real conditionals pp. 134, 211	Using pauses in public speaking p. 127	Language for presentations p. 127	People of all ages p. 132 Use background knowledge Make predictions Infer information Infer meaning Read for details Draw conclusions	State your opinion about a future event p. 134	Completing and talking about a lifestyle survey p. 129 Giving a speech about a solution to a problem p. 135
Wish statements pp. 146, 212 Negative modals pp. 152, 213	Word final /t/ and /d/ p. 152	Apologizing and accepting an apology p. 145	Money from unusual sources p. 150 Make predictions Read for details Infer meaning Compare and evaluate	Give an opinion on the best way to donate money p. 153	Renting an apartment p. 147 Persuading someone to donate money p. 153
Present unreal conditionals pp. 160, 214 Reported statements with *say* and *tell* pp. 166, 215	Repeating with rising intonation to show surprise p. 158	Giving strong advice p. 159	The kindness of strangers p. 164 Make connections Make predictions Sequence events Infer meaning	Describe a lie p. 167	Talking about dishonest actions p. 161 Explaining your actions p. 167
Embedded questions pp. 174, 216 The passive with various tenses pp. 180, 217	Negative questions to confirm information p. 177	Offering another opinion p. 173	When the seas rise p. 178 Use background knowledge Make predictions Take notes on key details Infer meaning Summarize Give opinions	Give an opinion on new construction p. 181	Taking a quiz about the world p. 175 Choosing a civic project p. 181

Language Summaries p. 186   Grammar Notes p. 193

1 INDOORS AND OUTDOORS

A couple relaxes in the Piazza Farnese, a public square in Rome, Italy.

Look at the photo. Answer the questions.

1 Where are the people in the photo?

2 Is there a public space like this in your city? Why do people gather there?

3 What is something you *shouldn't* do in public?

UNIT GOALS

1 Discuss home improvement ideas

2 Make and respond to informal suggestions

3 Talk about public versus private life

4 Discuss rules and appropriate behavior

1 VIDEO The Rise of Open Streets

A 🔄 What do you see in the photo? What do you think the video is going to be about? Tell a partner.

B ▶ Watch the beginning of the video. Check (✓) the things that are mentioned.

☐ dancing   ☐ getting a haircut   ☐ driving   ☐ walking

☐ catching the bus   ☐ practicing songs   ☐ yoga   ☐ playing soccer

C ▶ Watch the next part of the video and complete the sentences.

Open Streets are when you temporarily _____ a street to people _____ and then _____ it up for people _____, walking, skating, running—pretty much do anything but drive a car.

D ▶ Watch the full video and complete the quotes.

1. "You get young and old, _____ and _____, fat and skinny—you get everybody!"
2. "All you need is two _____ and a _____."
3. "Summer Streets celebrates the concept that streets are for _____."
4. "It's showing people that the streets can have different _____ according to the time of the _____, the day of the _____, the week of the _____..."
5. "It's a great way to bring in new folks who are maybe interested in _____ more and _____ more and adding more physical activity to their lifestyle but aren't sure how."

E 🔄 What do you think of Open Streets and events like it? Where would you create an open street in your city? Discuss with a partner.

2 VOCABULARY

Bright colors, when combined with neutral colors, create a wonderful look.

Word Bank
Words to describe a color *bright, dark, favorite, neutral, primary*

A 🔁 Two people are asking the Home Helper, a **home improvement** expert, for advice. Follow the instructions below.

Student A: Ask your partner question ❶.

Student B: Don't read the answer below. Give your own advice. Then switch roles and repeat for question ❷.

❶ *Dear Home Helper, We want to* **repaint** *our bedroom. I want to paint it my* **favorite color***: purple. My husband hates the idea. What do you think?*

Answer: **Dark colors** can make a room look smaller. Some colors, like orange and purple, can be **overwhelming** when used alone. **Combine** them with **neutral colors**, like beige and gray, when you **redo** your room.

❷ *Dear Home Helper, My sofa is broken, and the rest of my furniture doesn't* **work well** *in my apartment: it's too large. Should I* **get rid of** *all my furniture and start over?*

Answer: **Repair** your sofa, but you don't have to **replace** everything else. Have you tried **rearranging** your furniture? You may find a new **option** that works better for you and your room.

B 🔁 Now read the responses from the Home Helper. What is the advice? Is it similar to what you said in **A**? Do you agree with it? Tell your partner.

> I agree with her husband.
> Purple is a terrible choice.

ℹ️ The prefix *re-* can indicate that something is done in a second and, sometimes, different way.

rearrange   recreate   repaint

rebuild   redo   restart

Other words, like *replace* and *repair,* do not fit into this category.

C 🔁 Discuss the questions with a partner.

1. What works well in your bedroom right now? What doesn't?
2. What is one thing you would rearrange in your home?
3. You can repaint your bedroom any color. What color do you choose and why?
4. What colors go well together? What colors should not be combined?

3 LISTENING

A Look at the color wheel. Answer the questions with a partner.

1. When do you use a color wheel?

2. Which colors do you think are *warm*? Which ones are *cool*?

B **Pronunciation: Saying a series of items.** Read and listen to these sentences. Then listen and repeat. **CD 1 Track 2**

1. The three primary colors on the color wheel are red, yellow, and blue.

2. White, black, and gray are neutral colors.

3. Our living room has a sofa, table, and two chairs.

4. You can enlarge a space by using mirrors, light colors, and small furniture.

C Complete the chart below. Read and explain your answers to a partner.

> I really like red, yellow, and orange. They're my favorites because I like bright colors.

My three favorite colors

The three hardest subjects in school

My three favorite singers / actors

D **Make and check predictions.** You are going to hear a lecture about the color wheel. Read the chart and predict the answers. Then listen and complete the notes. **CD 1 Track 3**

What the color wheel does	shows us how to (1.) _____ colors in an attractive way
People who use the color wheel	painters, decorators, and (2.) _____ designers
Primary colors Use of these colors	red, (3.) _____, and (4.) _____ can (5.) _____ them together to create (6.) _____
Warm colors Their effect	yellow and (7.) _____ They have a lot of (8.) _____. They come (9.) _____ the viewer.
Cool colors Their effect	blue and (10.) _____ They are quiet and (11.) _____. They move (12.) _____ from the viewer.

E **Listen for details.** Listen to the information about combining colors. Which chart illustrates the speaker's point? **CD 1 Track 4**

1

2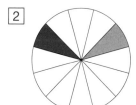

3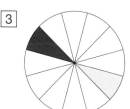

F Look back at your answers in **D**. Explain the lecture in your own words. What is your favorite color combination? Why? Tell a partner.

4 SPEAKING

A 🔊 Emilia has just moved into a new apartment. Listen to and read the conversation and answer the questions. **CD 1 Track 5**

1. How does Emilia like the apartment? What's the problem?

2. How does Felipe make suggestions to solve the problem? Underline the sentences.

3. How does Emilia accept and refuse the advice? Circle the sentences.

EMILIA: Thanks for your help, Felipe.

FELIPE: No problem. How do you like your new apartment?

EMILIA: It's great. I love it. There's just one thing...

FELIPE: Yeah?

EMILIA: I found a small crack in the wall.

FELIPE: The wall is cracked? Really?

EMILIA: Yeah. It's not too big, but it's in the living room, and everyone can see it.

FELIPE: Why don't you fix it yourself?

EMILIA: Um... I don't think so. I'm not good at repairing things.

FELIPE: I know! Try calling my friend, Sam. He can help you. He's a nice guy, and he's very capable.

EMILIA: That sounds like a great idea. Do you have his phone number?

FELIPE: Sure. Hold on a second while I get it...

B 🔄 Can you think of another way to solve Emilia's problem? What would you do? Tell your partner.

SPEAKING STRATEGY

C 🔄 Read the two situations. Choose one and role-play it with a partner. Then switch roles and role-play the other situation.

Student A: Tell your friend about your problem. Practice accepting and refusing suggestions.

Student B: Use the Useful Expressions to help you make suggestions.

Useful Expressions: Making informal suggestions	
With base form	With verb + *-ing*
Why don't you <u>fix</u> it yourself? I think you should <u>fix</u> it yourself.	Have you thought about <u>fixing</u> it yourself?
I know what you should do. <u>Call</u> my friend.	Try <u>calling</u> my friend.
Speaking tip	
You can respond to an informal suggestion with a strong or weak *yes* or a *no*.	

Problem: It's 2:00 AM. You return home and can't find the key to your house. You're locked out! Your roommate is sleeping and will be angry if you wake him.

Problem: You have just moved into a new apartment. It has very few windows and is dark. You don't have a lot of money to spend on home improvement.

ℹ️ **Responding:**
Strong yes: *Good idea! / That's a great idea. / Sounds good to me.*
Weak yes / maybe: *I guess it's worth a try. / Maybe I'll do that.*
No: *I don't think so. / No, I don't like that idea.*

5 GRAMMAR

A Turn to page 193. Complete the exercises. Then do **B–E** below.

Stative Passive Voice			
Subject	**Verb**	**Object**	
I	broke	the window.	This sentence describes an action.
Subject	**be**	**Past participle**	
The window	is	broken.	This sentence describes a state.

B Complete the chart with the correct forms of the verbs.

Base	Simple past	Past participle	Base	Simple past	Past participle
bend				flooded	
	broke		freeze		
clog			jam		
	cracked			stained	

C Complete the sentences with the correct form of the word in parentheses.

1. This room needs a lot of work. The walls (crack) _____ and the floor (stain) _____.
2. It rained a lot and now the basement (flood) _____.
3. Someone (break) _____ the window last week. I can't believe it _____ still (break) _____.
4. He (throw) _____ something into the sink. Now the drain (clog) _____.
5. This key doesn't work because it (bend) _____.

D Think of something in your home, your classroom, and your school that is broken or not working properly. Write the problems in the chart below.

	Problem	**Advice**	**Advice**
Home			
Classroom			
School			

E Tell two of your classmates about your three problems. Ask for their advice and write it in **D**. Which suggestions do you like? Why?

> A light bulb is burned out in our bathroom at home.

> Why don't you buy a new one and replace it?

6 COMMUNICATION

A Look at the photo of a room in an old hotel. Answer the questions with a partner.

1. Would you like to stay in this hotel? Why or why not?
2. What are some of the problems with this room?

B Read about a contest.

- A local company wants to restore the old hotel. They plan to start with the room in **A**. They are sponsoring a design contest.
- You are going to enter the design contest. Using the photo in **A**, come up with at least five ideas for improving the room.
- Your goals are to make the room more welcoming and comfortable.
- The winning design team will receive $25,000!

C Work with a partner. On a separate piece of paper, make a chart with two columns: *Ideas to make the room more welcoming* and *Ideas to make the room more comfortable.* Think of ideas for the design contest. Write them in the chart.

D Get together with another pair. Introduce yourselves and present your ideas to them. When you listen, take notes. Then explain what you like most about the other pair's design ideas.

Language for Presentations	
Introducing yourself	**Stating the purpose**
Hello, everyone. I'd like to thank you for coming. My name is... and I'm from (school / company).	Today, we're going to talk to you about...

The paparazzi are photographers who follow famous people and take pictures of them. They then sell the photos to websites and magazines.

1 VOCABULARY

A Look at the photo and read the information. Who are the paparazzi and what do they do? Why do they do it? Tell a partner.

B Read the opinions below. Match a person to each statement. Explain your choices to a partner.

a. My **private life** is my own. What I do in my free time is **no one else's business**.

c. I like to know any news about famous people right away! But I feel sorry for them. When they go out **in public**, the paparazzi follow them. Celebrities never **have** any **privacy**. That's hard.

b. Singers and actors are **public figures**. **The general public** is interested in them. It's natural to have paparazzi following them. I work with the paparazzi all the time.

d. Movie stars, like all people, have certain **rights**. For example, you can't **disturb** (= bother) them in their own homes.

1. Clark, entertainment blogger _____

2. Desiree, lawyer _____

3. Cesar, actor _____

4. Hong-li, student _____

C  Complete the phrases in the chart with words in **blue** from **B**. Then tell a partner: How are the *public* and *private* phrases different?

Opposites	
Public	**Private / Individual**
1. a public ____*figure*____	1. a private citizen
2. the _____	2. one person
3. (do something) _____	3. (do something) in private
4. your public life	4. your _____

A public figure is someone famous, like a movie star. But a private citizen...

D Which opinion(s) in **B** do you agree with? Why? Tell a partner.

2 LISTENING

A **Listen for main ideas.** You are going to listen to three conversations. Which statement (a, b, or c) is true about each conversation? Listen and circle the correct answer. **CD 1 Track 6**

1. a. The two friends are fighting.
   b. The boy wants to talk to the girl.
   c. The girl is talking to her boyfriend.

2. a. Paula is studying.
   b. Paula has met Carla Smith.
   c. Carla Smith is a public figure.

3. a. The woman is a singer.
   b. They are talking in private.
   c. They are meeting for the first time.

B **Infer information.** Read the sentences below. Then listen again. What might the person say next? Choose the best ending for each conversation. Two sentences are extra. **CD 1 Track 6**

Conversation 1 _____
Conversation 2 _____
Conversation 3 _____

a. She doesn't have any privacy. It's terrible!
b. They shouldn't speak to her in private like that. It's rude!
c. Sorry, but I don't talk about my private life on television.
d. Celebrities shouldn't do that in public.
e. Excuse me, but that's none of your business!

C What information do you share with friends and family? with classmates or coworkers? online? Tell a partner. Then say one thing you don't share.

I like to post pictures online, but I never talk about my private life.

3 READING

A **Make and check predictions.** Look at the photo and title. Then choose the best definition to complete the sentence. Read the article to check your answer.

A *landscape architect* _____.

a. designs parks and gardens
b. builds schools
c. gives tours

B  **Scan for information.** What three public spaces are talked about in the reading? Where are they? What do they have in common? Tell a partner.

C **Infer information.** Read again. Would the people agree or disagree with these statements? Check (✓) your answers. Underline the information that supports your answers.

1. **Jin Hee Park:** I'm always studying. I don't have time to appreciate the campus.
   ☐ agree   ☑ disagree

2. **Alejandro Vega:** Central Park is large, but it has a cozy feeling.
   ☐ agree   ☐ disagree

3. **Ross Howard:** Niagara Falls is totally open to the public.
   ☐ agree   ☐ disagree

4. **Olmsted:** We should keep the natural feeling of these places.
   ☐ agree   ☐ disagree

D **Read for details; Infer information.** Reread the last paragraph. Discuss the questions with a partner.

1. What place is talked about?
2. What problems is this place having?
3. How would you answer the question at the end?

CREATING PUBLIC SPACES

Central Park, New York City, US

Jin Hee Park is a student at Stanford University in California. She studies hard. "Of course, I came here for the academics," she says. "But it doesn't hurt that the campus is so beautiful. I walk around
5 sometimes just to relax."

Alejandro Vega, a banker in New York City, jogs almost every evening after work in Central Park. "I never get bored. The park is so big. It's got gardens, ponds, bike and walking paths,
10 restaurants, and beautiful architecture. And yet, in some places, it can feel completely private."

Niagara Falls was on Ross Howard's list of places to visit in upstate New York. "There are these wonderful footpaths in the park that make the
15 waterfalls so accessible to the general public. You can get really close. The walking paths near the falls are also great for hiking and picnics."

All of these people have one man to thank for these beautiful public spaces: Frederick Law
20 Olmsted. In 1858, a design contest was held for a new park in New York City. Olmsted and his partner, Calvert Vaux, won the contest. Central Park was the finished product—the first landscaped public park in the United States.
25 Today, no trip to New York is complete without a visit to this beautiful park.

Later in his life, Olmsted designed landscapes for college campuses, including Stanford University. He also designed footpaths at Niagara Falls to
30 give visitors better views of the falls. In all his work, Olmsted tried to preserve[1] the natural beauty of an area.

Today there are new pressures on Niagara Falls: some businesses want to develop the area. On
35 Goat Island, an island in Niagara Falls State Park, there are now souvenir shops. There may be signs that say *No Littering*,[2] but there is still a lot of trash on the island. And most of the animals have disappeared. If Olmsted could see these
40 changes, what would he think?

[1] To *preserve* is to save and protect
[2] To *litter* is to throw trash on the ground

4 GRAMMAR

A Turn to page 194. Complete the exercises. Then do **B** and **C** below.

Giving Permission and Expressing Prohibition				
	be	**allowed / permitted / supposed to**	**Base form**	
You	**are**(n't)	allowed to / permitted to	park	here.
		supposed to		
	Modal		**Base form**	
You	**can**('t)		park	here.
No	Gerund	**be**	**allowed / permitted**	
	Talking	**is**(n't)	allowed / permitted	during the test.
No	talking			

B  With a partner, write a rule for each public place using the language in the chart above.

Public transportation (a bus, the subway)

You're supposed to give your seat to an older person.

_____

A swimming pool

_____

A movie theater

_____

Your school or classroom

_____

C Get together with another pair. Take turns telling each other your rules in **B**. Do you always follow these rules? Why or why not?

> Running isn't allowed at a swimming pool.

> I never run at the pool, but some people do.

5 WRITING

A Read the list of items below. Then answer the questions with a partner.

1. Do you ever see people doing these things in public? Discuss.
2. What other annoying things do people do in public? Add two ideas.

Annoying things people do in public

Smoke

Cut the line in a store

Double park on the street

Eat on public transportation

Talk loudly on their phones

Litter

_____

_____

Word Bank
If something is *annoying*, it bothers or disturbs you.

B 🔁 Read the paragraph. Then answer the questions with a partner.

I hate it when people talk loudly on their phones in public. When you talk loudly on the phone, you disturb those around you. Yesterday, for example, I was on the bus, and the man near me was talking to his friend on the phone. I could hear everything, and his call continued for almost 15 minutes. I don't understand this kind of person. It's OK to talk on the phone, but you're supposed to do it quietly. The bus is a public space, and other people don't want to know your business. Some things aren't allowed on the bus, like eating and smoking. Sometimes, I think we should ban talking on the phone, too.

1. Which topic in **A** is the writer talking about? How does he feel about this behavior?

2. What example does he use to illustrate his opinion?

3. What does he think people should do about this problem?

C Choose a topic in **A** and answer the questions in **B** about it. Then use your notes and the example to help you write your own paragraph.

D 🔁 Exchange papers with a partner.

1. Circle any mistakes in your partner's paper. Answer the questions in **B** about your partner's paragraph.

2. Return the paper to your partner. Make corrections to your own paper.

6 COMMUNICATION

A 🔳 Work in a small group. Answer the questions with your group.

1. Look again at the list of annoying behaviors in Writing **A**. Are these behaviors allowed or not allowed by law in your country?

2. What do you think of these behaviors? Do you do any of them? How do you think they make people feel?

> You're not allowed to smoke in most indoor places.

> Yeah, but smoking is still permitted in some clubs. I hate it!

> I think people have the right to smoke in some public places.

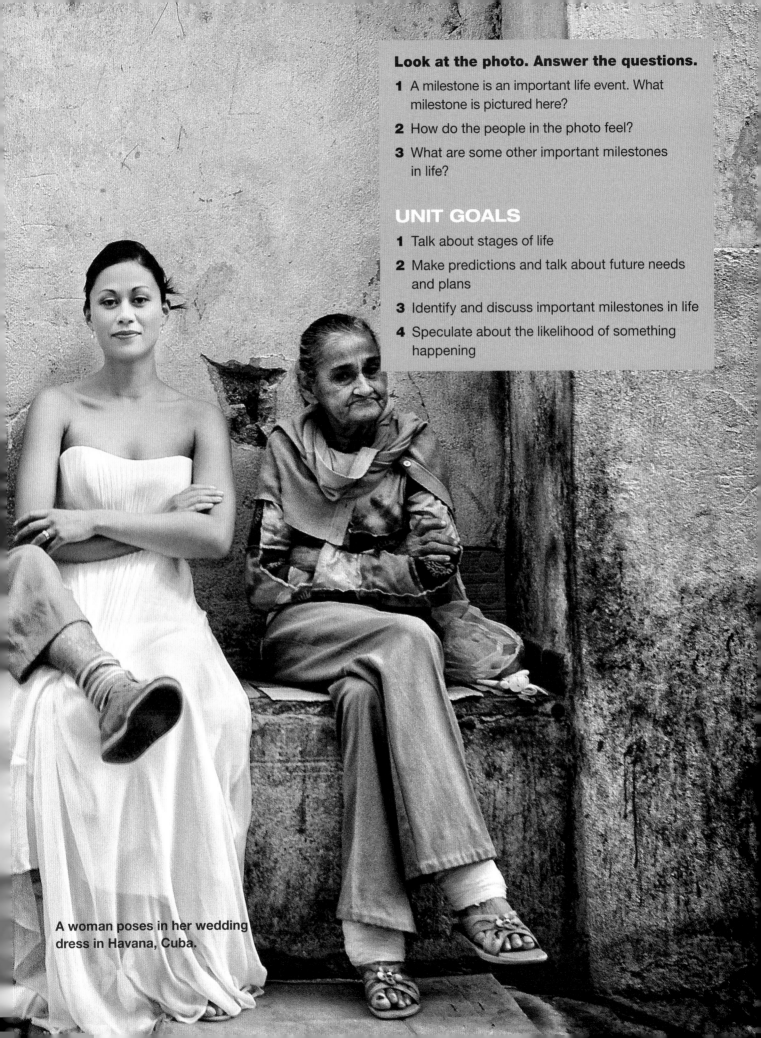

Look at the photo. Answer the questions.

1 A milestone is an important life event. What milestone is pictured here?

2 How do the people in the photo feel?

3 What are some other important milestones in life?

UNIT GOALS

1 Talk about stages of life

2 Make predictions and talk about future needs and plans

3 Identify and discuss important milestones in life

4 Speculate about the likelihood of something happening

A woman poses in her wedding dress in Havana, Cuba.

People in a retirement community

1 **VIDEO** I Like Being 98

Word Bank
retirement = when someone gets older and leaves working life
community = a group of people living together
retirement community = a place where older people live

A Read the information in the Word Bank. Why do you think some people "feel stuck" in retirement communities?

B ▶ Watch the first part of the video. Complete the information about Evelyn. What happened to her? How did she feel?

"I lost my _____ _____ because somebody thought I was too _____.
But I didn't have a mark against me at all. I was _____ at that, I really was. It made me feel old. It made me feel _____."

C ▶ Watch the full video. What do the words in *italics* refer to? Match them to the descriptions on the right. You will use one description twice.

1. We used to have a bus *here*. _____
2. They gave *it* up. _____
3. A lot of people were stuck around *here*. _____
4. Joyce didn't want to go *anywhere else*. _____
5. I went to get *it* back. _____
6. I passed *it*. _____
7. *That* will give you joy. _____
8. I don't do *this* so you think I'm great. _____

a. another place to live
b. bus to the supermarket
c. driver's license
d. help Joyce
e. driving test
f. loving your neighbor and being a friend
g. retirement community

D ⟳ What words describe Evelyn? Do you know anyone like her? Tell a partner.

2 VOCABULARY

| infant (baby) | toddler | child (kid) | adolescent (teenager) | adult (grown-up) |
| 0–18 months | 18 months–3 yrs | 3–12 | 13–19 | 20+ |

A How would you describe your relationship with your parents? Check (✓) the box. Explain your answer to a partner.

☐ We're all busy. We don't see each other that much.

☐ I think my parents are too strict. They should relax a little.

☐ We're like best friends. We talk about everything.

☐ other (your idea): _____

Word Bank

Stages
infancy → childhood →
adolescence → adulthood

B Read the article. What is it about?

- In a survey of 1,000 parents and 500 children, 43 percent of the **grown-ups** said they wanted to be their **children**'s "best friend."

- 40 percent said they wanted to buy their children everything they wanted.

Peggy, a parent with a 15-year-old **teenager**, said, "My **childhood** was difficult. We didn't have any money. I want to give my son everything he asks for."

Fred, a single dad, said, "**Adulthood** is all about responsibility. **Adolescence** is all about having fun. I don't want my children to work too hard."

Dr. Julio Garcia, a childcare specialist, says, "Children need an **adult** to rely on. They need rules—and a best friend isn't going to give you rules."

Interestingly, the **young adults** in the survey didn't share their parents' values.

- When they are ready to **start a family**, only 28 percent of them want to be their children's best friend.

- Only 10 percent want to buy their **kids** everything.

C Discuss the article in **B** with a partner. Then answer these questions.

1. Who do you agree with: Peggy, Fred, or Dr. Garcia?

2. When you are ready to start your own family, how will you raise your children?

3 LISTENING

A 🔊 **Pronunciation: Content word emphasis.** Listen to and repeat the following sentences. Notice how the underlined words are stressed. **CD 1 Track 8**

1. My <u>name</u> is <u>Deena Ravitch</u>, and I'm the <u>CEO</u> of <u>Symtax</u> <u>Corporation</u>.

2. I'm <u>happy</u> to be <u>here</u>.

3. <u>Today</u> is also a <u>time</u> to <u>look</u> to the <u>future</u>.

B 🔄 With a partner, take turns reading the sentences in **A**. Be sure to stress the content words.

Many skilled public speakers use inspiring sayings to move their audience.

C Look at the photo and read the caption. Do you know any inspiring sayings?

D 🔊 **Listen for gist.** You are going to hear a speech. Listen and answer the questions below. **CD 1 Track 9**

1. This speech is being given at a(n) _____.

    a. wedding   c. birthday celebration

    b. office party   d. graduation ceremony

2. What information in the speech helped you choose your answer? Write the key words below.

_____

E 🔊 **Listen for details.** Listen again to parts of the speech. What does the speaker mean when she says these things? **CD 1 Track 10**

1. "You are joining the work world with all its responsibilities. In short, you are leaving your comfort zone."

    a. You will face many unfamiliar situations.

    b. Your life will become more comfortable.

    c. It's not so difficult to find a job.

2. "No matter what, though, you were always driven to succeed. And now you are here today. Congratulations."

    a. Your classes were difficult and required a lot of thinking.

    b. You never gave up, and you should feel proud.

    c. You worried about today and not being successful.

3. "Shoot for the moon. Even if you miss it, you will land among the stars."

    a. Make a plan and ask for help.

    b. Travel a lot and experience new things.

    c. Try your hardest at everything you do.

F 🔄 Think about a speech that you heard or gave. Where were you? What was the speech about? Tell a partner.

4 SPEAKING

A 🔊 Listen to and read the conversation between Yuri and Max. Then read the three false statements about Max. Correct them and make them true. **CD 1 Track 11**

1. Max doesn't know how to drive.
2. His driver's license disappeared.
3. He's traveling in two days.

Getting a driver's license is an important milestone for many teenagers. To get a license, you need to pass a written test and take a driving test.

YURI: What are you studying for, Max?

MAX: Oh, hi, Yuri... just my driving test.

YURI: Your driving exam? Don't you have a driver's license already?

MAX: I had one... but it expired*, so I have to take the test again.

YURI: That's a drag.

MAX: Yeah, and I need to get my license soon.

YURI: How come?

MAX: I'm planning to visit my cousins in two weeks. I need to rent a car for the trip.

YURI: Sounds like fun. Well, good luck with everything!

* *expire* = to come to an end

B 🔄 Practice the conversation with a partner.

SPEAKING STRATEGY

C 🔄 What do you think these people's plans are? What do they need to do? Share your ideas with a partner. Use the Useful Expressions to help you.

Useful Expressions	
Talking about plans	
planning + infinitive	I'm planning to take a driving test.
going to + base form	I'm going to visit my cousins.
thinking about + gerund	I'm thinking about taking a trip.
Talking about needs	
need + infinitive	I need to rent a car.

D Check (✓) the items you plan to do in the future. Add one more item to the list.

- ☐ take a big trip
- ☐ apply for a credit card
- ☐ buy _____
- ☐ vote in an election
- ☐ move
- ☐ _____

E 🔄 Tell your partner what you plan to do and when. What do you need to do to make it happen?

5 GRAMMAR

A Turn to page 195. Complete the exercise. Then do **B** and **C** below.

Review of Future Forms	
Make a prediction	She **will go** to a good school. / She**'s going to go** to a good school. She**'s going to have** a baby.
State a future plan	The teenagers **are going to work** part time this summer. The teenagers **are working** part time this summer.
Scheduled events	The kids **are going to go** / **are going** / **go** to summer camp on August 2nd.

> **i** Use *will* for quick decisions / offers: (phone ringing) *I'll get it!*

B Unscramble the questions.

1. you'll / think / a / do / life / you / have / happy

   _____?

2. happen / what / think / going / to / is / do / you / week / next

   _____?

3. how / the / life / in / different / will / future / be

   _____?

4. today / does / time / class / what / end

   _____?

5. doing / you / this / for / vacation / what / year / are

   _____?

6. are / what / this / to / weekend / you / do / going

   _____?

C 🔁 Work with a partner. Take turns asking and answering the questions in **B**.

> What are you doing for vacation this year?

> I'm going to go to Cozumel!

Cozumel, Mexico

6 COMMUNICATION

> The Magic Answer Bag can predict your future. You ask it a question and then reach in and pull out your answer.

A In groups of three or four, write each expression from the box below on a slip of paper and fold each paper. Each group puts their papers in a bag or hat.

Yes	No	Maybe
Absolutely!	No way!	It's possible.
For sure!	Not a chance!	Maybe.
Of course!	It's not going to happen!	Who knows?

B What would you like to know about your future? Think of four *Yes / No* questions and write them down. Do not show anyone yet.

Example: _Will I get a good grade on my next exam?_

1. _____

_____

2. _____

_____

3. _____

_____

4. _____

_____

C You are now going to get answers to your questions. Ask the Magic Answer Bag your first question. A member of your group should shake the bag, pull out an answer, and read it aloud. Write your answer below the question in **B**. Take turns asking your questions.

> Will I get a good grade on my next exam?

> I'm sorry. The answer is "No way!"

People in some countries also use colorful picture playing cards (called *tarot cards*) to get answers about the future.

D Discuss the Magic Answer Bag's answers. Do you think they were accurate? Why or why not?

1 VOCABULARY

A Match the words in column A with those in B. Then read the story about Fran Turner. Use the expressions to complete the story. (Remember to use the past tense if necessary!)

A	B
be get have	born married children divorced

At first, Fran Turner's life wasn't so different. Like many people, she **fell in love** and (1.) _____. Fran **got pregnant** and the couple (2.) _____ two _____. She and her husband **bought a house**. Fran **got a job** as a lawyer's assistant while she also **raised her family**. She was your typical "working mom."

Over the years, things changed. One of Fran's daughters graduated from high school. Another **left home** and **enrolled** in college. Fran **went to school** and studied journalism. Fran and her husband also began to grow apart. She never really expected to (3.) _____—but her marriage ended.

Fran (4.) _____ in 1952. And in 1998, at the age of 46, she decided to take a trip to Central America. Fran realized that she liked traveling. For the last 20 years, she has traveled around the world, meeting new people, learning about new cultures, and writing about her experiences for travel magazines. She loves it, and probably is not going to **retire** anytime soon!

B Look again at the expressions in blue in **A**. When do these events typically happen in one's life: childhood, adolescence, or adulthood? Complete the rest of the box with present tense forms.

childhood	
adolescence	
adulthood	

C 🔁 Don't look at **A**. Use the expressions in **B** to retell Fran's story with a partner.

2 LISTENING

A Look at the **blue** vocabulary words on page 24. Which of life's events are you looking forward to? Which ones do you want to avoid? Tell a partner.

B 🔊 **Listen for gist.** Lindsay is reading a magazine quiz. Listen and choose the best title for the quiz. **CD 1 Track 12**

    a. Is Your Life Happy?

    b. How Can You Get the Best Job?

    c. Which Life Event is the Most Exciting?

    d. Are You a Happy Teen?

C 🔊 **Listen for details.** Listen. Check (✓) the life event each person chooses. Write key words that explain the reasons for the person's answer. **CD 1 Track 13**

Person	Event		Reasons
Mark	☐ get a job	☐ leave home	_____
Lindsay	☐ get married	☐ have a big family	_____
Dad	☐ get a promotion	☐ retire	_____

D Who are you most similar to: Mark, Lindsay, or their dad? Tell a partner.

3 READING

A 🔄 **Make predictions.** Read the title and look at the photo. What do you think this man does? Tell a partner. Then read the article to check your ideas.

B **Infer meaning.** Match the words in *italics* in the article with the correct definitions below.

1. a talk given to teach people something _____
2. disagreed _____
3. a group of people with a specific purpose _____
4. communicate an idea _____
5. nature _____

C 🔄 **Scan for details.** Find answers to the questions and underline them in the article. Ask and answer the questions with a partner. Answer in your own words.

1. Why did John stop using cars?
2. Why did he stop talking?
3. What did John learn by not talking? What did he teach people?
4. What places did John visit? How did he get to them?
5. Why did John start talking again?
6. What things did he do after he started talking again?

D 🔄 Discuss with a partner.

1. Do you think John's walk has helped the environment?
2. Have you ever experienced a "life-changing event"? What happened? How did the event change your life?

WORLD LINK

Plan a planet walk in your country. Where will you go? What will the message be?

JOHN FRANCIS:
THE PLANET WALKER

John Francis was born in 1946, in Philadelphia, in the United States, but in his early twenties, he left home and moved to the San Francisco area. In many ways, John's life in his new city was pretty typical. He got a job and made friends. He planned for his future. But then, two years after he arrived, something happened, and the event changed John's life forever. One day, there was a big oil spill[1] that caused a lot of damage to the local *environment*. The spill killed hundreds of animals and polluted the water in the area terribly. John was so upset by this that he decided to stop using automobiles altogether. Instead, he started walking everywhere.

When John told people he didn't ride in cars, people *argued* with him. John didn't like to fight, so he decided to stop talking for an entire day. One day became two, two days turned into a week, and finally, John decided to stop talking completely. After several weeks, he discovered something: He realized that he didn't always listen to people. By not talking, he started to really hear what others had to say.

John remained silent for 17 years. During this time, he tried to teach others about protecting the environment. He was in the newspaper several times, and he even gave *lectures* at universities. Although he didn't talk, John was still able to *get his message across* to listeners. He explained his ideas through hand motions, paintings, and the music of his banjo.

[1]If there is an *oil spill*, oil comes out of a ship and goes into the water.

John eventually enrolled in college (he walked hundreds of kilometers to get there), and he got a degree in environmental studies. After he graduated, John continued his journey around the United States. He also traveled on foot and by boat to South America, the Caribbean, and other places around the world, trying to educate people about caring for the environment and each other.

John wanted to share his story with more people, so in 1990 he started to talk again. John also started to ride in cars, but his work continued. He helped write environmental laws, worked for the United Nations as a goodwill ambassador, and started Planetwalk, an *organization* that helps raise awareness[2] for environmental and humanitarian[3] issues. He also started working with National Geographic.

Today, John Francis is still trying to make the world a better place. He has written a book to inspire a new generation of planetwalkers. In it, he explains how anyone can make their own walk. He also continues to teach people about the environment. The environment, he says, is not just about animals and plants. It's about how we treat each other. If we're going to make the world a better place, we need to do it for each other, not just ourselves.

[2]To *raise awareness* is to bring attention to something.
[3]*Humanitarian* issues have to do with improving human lives.

4 GRAMMAR

A Turn to page 196. Complete the exercises. Then do **B** and **C** below.

Modals of Future Possibility			
Subject	**Modal**	**Main verb**	
I / He / They	**may / might / could**	go	to college in the fall.
	may / might not		

Yes / No questions and short answers			
With *be*	Will you <u>be</u> home by midnight?	I **may / might / could be.** I **may / might not be.**	I don't know. I'm not sure.
With other verbs	Are you going to <u>go</u> to college?	I **may / might / could.** I **may / might not.**	It's hard to say right now. We'll see.

Remember: If you are certain about something in the future, answer like this:

Will you be home by midnight? Yes, I will. or No, I won't.

Are you going to go to college? Yes, I am. or No, I'm not.

B How possible is it that the predictions below will come true in your lifetime? Complete the sentences with *will / won't*, *may / might (not)*, or *could*. Then add two ideas of your own.

1. Scientists _____ solve the global warming problem.

2. World hunger _____ end.

3. We _____ travel to other planets.

4. The world's population _____ decrease (go down).

5. _____ .

6. _____ .

C Work in a small group. Take turns asking about the situations in **B**. Each person should explain his or her answers.

> Will scientists solve the global warming problem in our lifetime?

> They probably won't. A lot of people still drive cars and use oil.

> They could. Many countries are working on it. We'll see.

As our planet warms, hurricanes and other storms are becoming stronger in some places.

5 WRITING

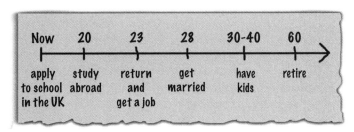

Now	20	23	28	30-40	60
apply to school in the UK	study abroad	return and get a job	get married	have kids	retire

What will my future be like? It's hard to know for sure, but I do have some plans. **This year,** for example, I'm going to apply to the London School of Economics. I want to study there **next year.** I hope I get accepted! If this happens, I want to spend two years in the UK. **Then,** when I'm 23, I may come home and look for a job, or I might stay in the UK. It's hard to know. **Later,** when I'm 28...

> ℹ Notice how the writer uses the words in bold to explain a sequence of events.

A Look at the timeline and read about one person's plans for the future. What things...

1. is the writer definitely going to do?

2. may or may not happen?

B Make a future timeline of your own. Put at least five events on it. List things that you know *will* happen and some that *may* happen. Then use your notes and the example to help you write your own paragraph. Use the words from the example to show a sequence.

C 🔁 Exchange papers with a partner.

1. Circle mistakes in your partner's paper. Answer the questions in **A** about your partner's plans.

2. Return the paper to your partner. Make corrections to your own paper.

6 COMMUNICATION

A Complete the quiz about your future life.

	I may / might	I will	I won't
1. have at least three children			
2. get married more than once			
3. retire in 30 years			
4. graduate early			
5. get a promotion			
6. live alone			
7. travel somewhere fun or exciting			
8. see or meet a famous person			
9. get a job using English			
10. get a driver's license			
11. leave home before age 20			
12. buy a home			

B 🔁 Interview your partner. Ask and answer questions about events in the chart above.

> Will you have at least three children?

> I know I won't. It's challenging to raise a large family.

C 👥 Join another pair. Explain how you are similar to or different from each other.

3 GETTING INFORMATION

Look at the photo. Answer the questions.

1 Where are these people?

2 What do you think they're talking about?

3 What do you talk about most often with your friends?

UNIT GOALS

1 Identify who someone is and where something is

2 Interrupt someone politely

3 Talk about how you get news and information

4 Share recent news about yourself and others

People talk at a cafe in Montevideo, Uruguay.

Pocahontas County, West Virginia

1 VIDEO A Unique US Town

A The video is about a town in a *quiet zone*. What do you think a quiet zone is?

B ▶ What do people say about life in Green Bank, West Virginia? Watch the video and complete the sentences.

1. "Just listen to _____ all around you."

2. "No one here has a _____."

3. "There's a long list of _____ conveniences that we can't utilize here."

4. "We can't _____ because I don't have service."

5. "I really enjoy it because it's _____, it's peaceful, it's _____."

C 🔄 Would you want to live in a quiet zone? Why or why not? Tell a partner.

2 VOCABULARY

When we were younger, my brother and I **argued** a lot...

...but now we **share** everything. We have great **conversations**.

Word Bank				
Verbs				**Nouns**
argue converse chat gossip talk[1]	<u>with</u> *someone* <u>about</u> *something*	get into an ~ strike up / start a ~, carry on a ~ have[2] a ~, stop by for a ~ a ~ of (the plan) give a ~, listen to a ~		argument conversation chat discussion talk
discuss share	*something* <u>with</u> *someone*	the latest ~, juicy ~, a piece of ~		**gossip**

[1]You can also *talk <u>to</u> someone.*

[2]*Have* can also be used before *argument, conversation, discussion,* and *talk.*

A 🔁 Look at the verbs in the Word Bank. All of them are related to talking. Answer the questions with a partner.

> What does "argue" mean?
>
> It means to fight or disagree with someone when you are talking.

1. How are the verbs similar? How are they different? Ask your partner. Use your dictionary to help you if necessary.

2. Which verbs have a negative meaning? Circle them.

3. Which verbs have an identical noun form? Underline them.

B 🔁 Ask and answer the questions with a partner.

1. When is the last time you **got into an argument** with someone? Who was it with? What was it about?

2. Are you good at **striking up conversations** with people you don't know well? Why or why not?

3. How often do you **chat** with your neighbors?

4. Think of a well-known celebrity. What is **one piece of** juicy **gossip** about him or her?

5. What is one thing you want to **discuss** with your instructor?

6. Who do you **share** your personal thoughts with? Why do you choose that person?

7. Who do you **talk to** on a daily basis? What do you **talk about**?

> I got into an argument with my mom yesterday. She's always telling me to clean my room!

3 LISTENING

A  Look at the names of the websites below with a partner. Add one more. Which one(s) do you know? Which one(s) do you use?

Facebook   Qzone   Twitter
Instagram   LinkedIn   Mixi
Sina Weibo
our idea: _____

B 🔊 **Infer information.** Read the questions. Then listen to an advertisement for a new online service. Which question might you ask with the service? **CD 1 Track 15**

a. Do you own a phone?

b. Can I borrow your phone?

c. What's an affordable phone?

d. What's the best thing about phones?

C 🔊 **Listen for details.** Listen again. Complete the summary about InstaHelp and how it works. **CD 1 Track 15**

When you have a question, it's easy to waste time looking for (1.) _____ online.

InstaHelp is an (2.) _____ service. You ask an important (3.) _____ by

(4.) _____ or instant message. InstaHelp (5.) _____ it on to some of your online

(6.) _____ (and their acquaintances, too). You then get live answers back in

(7.) _____ minutes or so.

D  Look back at your answers in **C** and explain to a partner how the InstaHelp service works. Would you use it? Why or why not?

E 🔊 **Pronunciation: Stress: Verb + preposition.** Look at the two underlined words in each question. Which one is stressed? Circle it. Listen and check your answers. **CD 1 Track 16**

1. Who do you <u>talk</u> <u>to</u> when you have a problem?

2. What do you <u>talk</u> <u>about</u> with your friends?

3. What is everyone <u>gossiping</u> <u>about</u> these days?

4. Do you need to <u>discuss</u> anything <u>with</u> your teacher?

5. Who do you <u>chat</u> <u>with</u> the most on the phone?

F  Practice saying the questions in **E**. Ask and answer the questions with a partner.

4 SPEAKING

A 🔊 Listen to and read the conversation. Answer the questions. **CD 1 Track 17**

1. What does Jared need?

2. What is Ana's advice?

3. Does Jared know Ms. Ruiz? How do you know?

ANA: Oh, look... there's Gloria Ruiz. Do you know her?

JARED: No, I don't. Who is she?

ANA: She's the VP of Marketing for Global Industries. She's standing right over there.

JARED: Is she the tall woman in the sweater?

ANA: No, Gloria is the woman with glasses. She's chatting with the man in the suit.

JARED: You know, I *am* looking for a job.

ANA: You should talk to her. Maybe she can help you.

JARED: That's a good idea. Thanks!

....

JARED: Excuse me, Ms. Ruiz? May I interrupt for a moment? My name is Jared Levy....

B 🔁 Practice the conversation with a partner.

SPEAKING STRATEGY

C 🔁 Think of a time you interrupted someone. Who were you talking to? What were you talking about? Tell a partner.

> My friend and I were having a discussion about our homework. I interrupted because my bus was coming!

D 👥 Role-play. Work in groups of three. Use the Useful Expressions to help you.

Student 1: You are at a party. You need to interrupt two people who are having a conversation. Choose a reason below.

- You think you know Student 2. You want to introduce yourself.

- You need directions from the party to another place.

- Your idea: _____

_____

_____

Useful Expressions: Interrupting someone politely
Introducing yourself
Excuse me. May I interrupt for a moment? My name is...
I'm sorry to interrupt. / I beg your pardon.
I just wanted to introduce myself. My name is...
Interrupting someone you know
Excuse me. Sorry to bother you, (name), but I have a question.
Could I interrupt for a second? I just wanted to say / ask something.

Students 2 and 3: You are chatting. Student 1 will interrupt your conversation. Ask him or her at least two questions.

5 GRAMMAR

A Turn to page 197. Complete the exercises. Then do **B–D** below.

Participial and Prepositional Phrases		
Who is Joe Ortega?	He's the guy	**chatting on the phone.** **on the phone.**
Who is Ms. Anh?	She's the woman	**wearing glasses.** **in front of the class.**
Which books are mine?	They're the ones	**lying on the floor.** **in the drawer.**

Prepositions

against the wall
alongside the house
between the desks
by the road
in the suit
on the table
opposite the door
under(neath) the tree
with the glasses

B Match the questions with their answers. Then use the words in the box to complete the answers with the correct prepositions and verb forms.

argue	between	discuss	hide	~~in~~	in
in	on	~~play~~	with	with	under

1. Who's the leader of the band?
2. Which one is your sister?
3. Which one is my package?
4. Which one is your cat?
5. Who are your friends?
6. Who's Tom?

a. He's the student _____ his grade _____ the instructor.
b. He's the guy __in__ the hat __playing__ the guitar.
c. They're the people _____ the cafe _____ about politics.
d. She's the girl _____ the ponytail _____ the skateboard.
e. It's the one _____ _____ the bed.
f. It's the one _____ the hall _____ the two tables.

C Work with a partner. Follow the steps to play a guessing game.

1. Think of an object and a person that you can see in your classroom. Don't tell your partner!

2. Ask *Yes / No* questions to identify your partner's object and person.

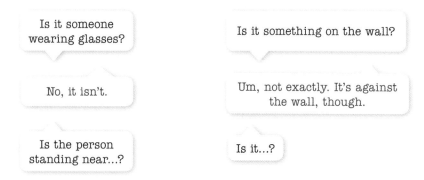

Is it someone wearing glasses?

No, it isn't.

Is the person standing near...?

Is it something on the wall?

Um, not exactly. It's against the wall, though.

Is it...?

D Switch roles and play the game again.

6 COMMUNICATION

A What do the quotes mean? Discuss with a small group. Share your ideas with the class.

"Great minds discuss ideas. Average minds discuss events. Small minds discuss people."
—Eleanor Roosevelt

"Never argue with stupid people. They will drag you down to their level and then beat you with experience." —Mark Twain

"Silence is one of the great arts of conversation." —Chinese proverb

B Think about the ways you communicate. Do you agree with any of these quotes? Explain your opinions to a partner.

C Read the situations below. Which behaviors bother you the most? Put them in order from 1 (most annoying) to 5 (least annoying).

A person / People…

_____ talking loudly on the phone on the train.

_____ having an argument in a restaurant.

_____ gossiping loudly about someone else.

_____ chatting during a movie.

_____ discussing sensitive political issues during dinner.

> Which situation is most annoying to you?

> It's definitely when a person talks loudly on the phone on the train. That behavior really bothers me!

D Form a small group. Tell your group members your answers for the most and least annoying behaviors in **C**. Explain your answers.

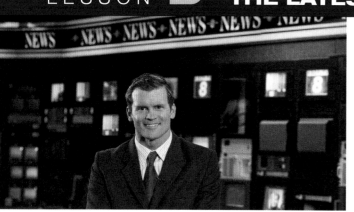

1 VOCABULARY

A  Look at the words below in blue. Are there any you don't know? Work with a partner to learn their meanings. Then take the quiz on your own.

1. How do you typically **get your news**?   ☐ TV   ☐ radio   ☐ online   ☐ other

2. I am most interested in... because _____.

   ☐ **international** (world) **news**   ☐ **local news** (about my town or city)

   ☐ **national news** (about my country)

3. What's one popular **news program** or **news site** in your country? _____

   What kind of news show or site is it?

   entertainment / **international** / **local** / **national** / **sports** / **tabloid** news

   Do you ever watch this news program or visit the site? _____

4. When you read an interesting news **story**, do you post it online? _____

5. Think of someone famous who was **in the news** recently. Who was it? _____

   Was the news about this person **bad**, **good**, **great**, **sad**, or **sensational**? _____

   Did the news about the person **spread** from place to place quickly? _____

6. Think again about the **news story** in #5. How did you **hear the news**?

   ☐ on TV   ☐ on the radio   ☐ on social media   ☐ online

   ☐ by **word of mouth** (= someone told me)

   Did you **tell anyone** else **the news**? If so, how many people did you tell? _____

B Explain your quiz answers to a partner.

> How do you typically get your news?

> Usually online, I guess. I never watch TV.

2 LISTENING

A  **Make predictions.** You will hear two reporters talk about three stories that were in the news recently. Which one (a, b, or c) do you think most people wanted to read or hear about? Circle your answer and then tell a partner.

a. news about jobs and the economy

b. the president's meeting in Asia

c. a scandal involving a soccer player

B **Check predictions.** Listen and check your answer in **A**. CD 1 Track 18

C **Listen for details; Infer information.** Read the sentences. Then listen to the full conversation and circle *True* or *False*. Correct the false sentences. CD 1 Track 19

1. The woman feels that a lot of news today is too sensational. True False

2. The man says news today is trying to educate the public. True False

3. The man says the least popular news stories are about murder and sports. True False

4. The woman believes there should be more news about the economy and the environment. True False

D Discuss the questions with a partner.

1. Do you agree with the opinions in **C**? Why?

2. Think of a story that was in the news a lot recently. Do you think it was important? Why or why not? How long was it in the news?

3 READING

A ⚡ **Use background knowledge.** Look at the title. What is a viral news story? Can you think of one example? Tell a partner.

B ⚡ **Sequence events.** Read the first news story. Number the events in the order they happened. Then retell the story to a partner using the appropriate verb forms.

a. _____ Lulu barks like a dog.

b. _____ Lulu is adopted.

c. _____ Ken is unconscious.

d. _____ The family finds Ken.

e. _____ Lulu goes everywhere with Ken.

f. _____ Lulu's mother dies.

g. _____ Ken has an accident.

C ⚡ **Make connections.** Read the second news story. What do these pairs of items have in common? Write your answers and then compare them with a partner's.

1. visit waterfalls / go horseback riding
   These are things you can do in Vanuatu.

2. scuba diving / snorkeling _____
   _____

3. three meters below the surface / near Port Vila _____
   _____

4. buy waterproof postcards / receive a special stamp _____
   _____

D ⚡ **Summarize.** Why do you think each news story went viral? Give a reason for each story. Discuss with a partner.

A *viral news* story spreads quickly, usually online, and becomes very popular.

Lulu to the Rescue!

Lulu is a kangaroo. For ten years she has lived with the Richards family. Lulu was adopted by the family after they found her next to her dead mother, not far from the Richards family's home in New South Wales, Australia.

Ken Richards is a farmer. He was working on his farm when a heavy tree branch suddenly fell on top of him and he passed out.[1]

Lulu stood next to Mr. Richards's body. She started barking and didn't leave Mr. Richards's side.

"I've never heard Lulu bark like that—she sounded like a dog. She barked and barked, and she didn't stop," said Celeste, Mr. Richards's daughter.

After 15 minutes, the Richards family went to investigate.[2] They found Ken on the ground.

"Lulu is a hero," said Celeste. "She saved my father."

Craig Middleton, a veterinarian, says that Lulu's story is rare. "I have never seen a kangaroo act like that. Maybe Lulu helped Ken Richards because the Richards family is the only family she has ever known."

Lulu is a loyal, friendly, and very intelligent kangaroo. After Ken leaves the hospital, he is planning to go everywhere with Lulu.

This Post Office is All Wet

The Republic of Vanuatu has recently been in the news—but not for the usual reasons.

Approximately 175,000 people live in the Republic of Vanuatu, an island chain east of Australia. It is a popular tourist destination because there's a lot to do there: you can visit waterfalls, go horseback riding, or visit a traditional Ni-Vanuatu village. Vanuatu is most famous for its scuba diving and snorkeling.

In an effort to draw attention to these popular water sports, Vanuatu has created a world's "first": the government has opened an underwater post office. You have to be a trained scuba diver to work there. The office is three meters below the surface in an area outside Port Vila, the capital city.

So far, the post office has hired four workers. They will work in a room surrounded by the beauty of Vanuatu's underwater world. Customers will buy waterproof postcards on land and then dive down to the post office to receive a special waterproof stamp!

[1]If you *pass out*, you fall down and lose consciousness.
[2]If you *investigate* something, you look at it carefully.

4 GRAMMAR

A Turn to page 198. Complete the exercise. Then do **B–D** below.

					Review of the Present Perfect
Question word	*have / has*	**Subject**	**Past participle**		**Answers**
Have	you	heard	the news?		Yes, I **have**. I heard it this morning.* No, I **haven't**. What happened?
How long	**have**	you	been	a reporter?	(I've **been** a reporter) **for** six months.
	has	she			(She's **been** a reporter) **since** May.

*When you answer a present perfect question with a specific time expression, use <u>the simple past</u>:
Have you heard the news? Yes, I <u>heard</u> it <u>this morning</u>.

B Unscramble the questions.

1. read / you / any funny / have / recently / news stories

   _____

2. in English / ever / have / you / watched / the news

   _____

3. studied / how long / you / English / have

   _____

4. studied / another / have / language / ever / you

   _____

5. known / your best friend / have / you / how long

   _____

C 🔁 Ask and answer the questions in **B** with a partner. Write your partner's answers below. Then ask a follow-up question.

Example: *Yoshi has known his best friend for ten years. They met in elementary school.*

1. _____
2. _____
3. _____
4. _____
5. _____

> So you've known your best friend for ten years. Where did you meet?

> In elementary school.

D 🔺 Tell another pair one thing you learned about your partner.

5 WRITING

A Read the message Sofia sent to her college roommate Emma.

1. Are the underlined words correct or not? Find the three mistakes and correct them.

2. Answer the questions about Sofia:

   a. Where does Sofia live? How long has she been there?

   b. What does she do? How long has she had this job?

   c. Is Sofia married or dating anyone? If yes, how long have they been together?

Hey Emma,

How are you? <u>I haven't seen</u> you in a long time. What are you doing these days? A lot <u>has changed</u> for me <u>since</u> college. At the moment, I'm living in Barcelona. <u>I'm</u> here <u>since</u> three years, and I really like it. I came to Barcelona to go to graduate school. I <u>finished</u> three months ago, and I've just gotten a job at a local TV station. It's cool. In other news, I <u>haven't meet</u> anyone special, so I'm still single. What's new with you? Are you going to our class reunion next month? Let me know!

Sofia

> **Word Bank**
>
> Use *in other news* to change from talking about one topic to a different one.
>
> At a *class reunion*, people from the same graduating class get together and have a party. Usually the people haven't seen each other for a long time.

B Imagine it's ten years in the future and you are doing something interesting in your life. Answer questions 2a–c in **A** about your future life. Use the present perfect tense. Then use your notes and the example to help you write an email to a classmate.

C 🔄 Exchange papers with a partner.

1. Circle any mistakes in your partner's email. Answer questions 2a–c in **A** about your partner.

2. Return the paper to your partner. Make corrections to your own email.

Park Güell, Barcelona

6 COMMUNICATION

A 👥 Imagine it's ten years in the future and you are at a class reunion. Talk to six different people and find out what they're doing these days. Use your notes from Writing.

B 🔄 Think about the people at the reunion. Which of your classmates has changed the most? Tell a partner.

> So, what's new, Sofia?

> A lot. I'm living in Barcelona now.

> No way! How long have you been there?

1 STORYBOARD

A Talia bought something at a furniture store. She is returning to the store. Look at the pictures and complete the conversations. More than one answer is possible for each blank.

B Practice the conversations in groups of three. Then change roles and practice again.

2 SEE IT AND SAY IT

A 🔁 Look at the picture below. Answer the questions with a partner.

1. Where are the people?

2. What are they doing? Why are they doing it?

B 🔁 With a partner, describe what each person is planning to do in the future. Say as much as you can about each person's plans.

> Daisuke is thinking about buying a houseboat. He wants to live on the water. He's probably going to become an artist.

C 🔁 Tell a new partner about your future plans. Where are you going to live? What kind of work are you going to do?

3 GET AND HAVE

A Follow the steps below.

1. Match the words in A, B, and C to make expressions with *get* and *have*.

2. Write your answers in the chart below.

3. Use the column letters (A, B, and C) in the chart as clues to help you.

A	B	C
get have	a divorced into married your	baby an argument friendly chat happy childhood news

get	have
(A + B) _____ *get divorced* _____	(A + B + C) _____
(A + B) _____	(A + B + C) _____
(A + B + C) _____	(A + B + C) _____
(A + B + C) _____	(A + C) _____

B Compare your answers with a partner's.

C Take turns choosing an expression in **A**. Make a sentence using that expression.

4 LISTENING

A Listen as John and Amy talk about the photo. Use the names in the box to label the people.
CD 1 Track 21

a. ~~John~~	d. Joseph
b. Olivia	e. Randy
c. Tina	f. Tom

B 🔊 Listen again. Complete the chart about where the people are now. **CD 1 Track 21**

Joseph and Olivia	They are _____ now. Olivia lives in _____. Joseph is _____ in Florida.
Randy	He just had _____.
Tom	He just _____.
Tina	She's _____ high school.

C 👥 Do you have a photo of family members in your wallet or on your phone? Show your photo to the class and talk about it.

> The person standing in front of me is my sister. Her name is...

5 SWIMMING POOL RULES

A 🔄 Look at the picture. Take turns saying the rules at the swimming pool. Point to the people breaking the rules. What are they doing?

> No dogs are allowed in the pool.

B 👥 Make up a list of rules for your classroom and share them with the class.

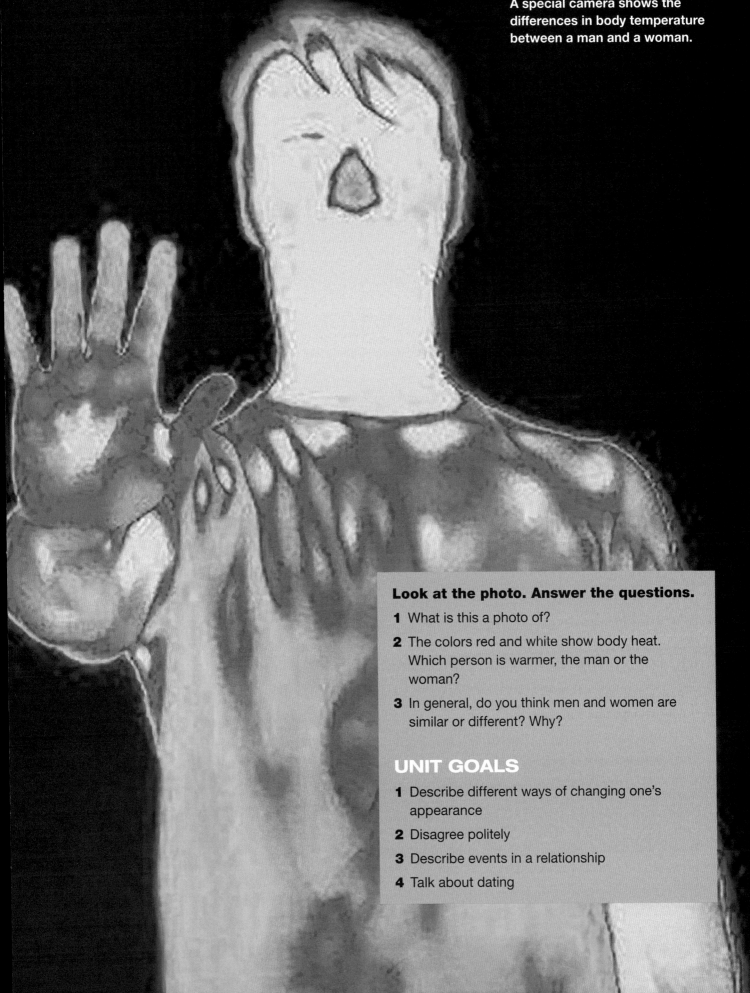

A special camera shows the differences in body temperature between a man and a woman.

Look at the photo. Answer the questions.

1 What is this a photo of?

2 The colors red and white show body heat. Which person is warmer, the man or the woman?

3 In general, do you think men and women are similar or different? Why?

UNIT GOALS

1 Describe different ways of changing one's appearance

2 Disagree politely

3 Describe events in a relationship

4 Talk about dating

1 **VIDEO** Battle of the Sexes

A Do you think you're a good listener? Why or why not? Discuss with a partner.

B Watch the first part of the video. Don't write anything, just watch.

C Before you watch the full video, try to choose the correct answers.

1. The man's name is _____.	a. Tom	b. Todd	c. Thad
2. The woman's name is _____.	a. Jane	b. Jen	c. Jill
3. What kind of pets do they own?	a. dog	b. bird	c. both
4. What does the wife do for a living?	a. teacher	b. mother	c. both
5. What did the wife say she was better at?	a. playing tennis	b. grilling	c. remembering details
6. What sport do they play?	a. soccer	b. tennis	c. golf

D Watch the full video and check your answers in **C**. What is the conclusion at the end of the video? Circle your answer below. Do you agree or disagree? Tell a partner.

a. Women are better listeners.   b. Men are better listeners.   c. Men and women listen differently.

2 VOCABULARY

A Use the verbs in the box to complete the descriptions. Which description was probably said by a woman? Which was said by a man? Are either of them true for you?

get	wash	wear	shave	brush

1. I ___wash___ my hair every day. Sometimes I _____ makeup, but I don't _____ perfume.

2. I _____ a haircut pretty often, and I _____ every couple of days, but I don't like to _____ my hair. I like it to look a little messy.

B Look at the Word Bank on the left. Use your dictionary to look up any unfamiliar words. Then match the verbs on the left with as many nouns as possible on the right. Make a list of the phrases you form on a piece of paper.

Word Bank		
brush		ears pierced
color / dye		face
get	your	hair
shave		head
straighten		teeth

Word Bank
Other expressions
get a (haircut / manicure / tattoo)
wear (cologne / deodorant / makeup / perfume)

C Discuss the questions with a partner.

1. When do you brush your teeth?

2. Imagine you are going to dye your hair. What color do you choose and why?

3. Where do you get your hair cut? How much does it cost? How often do you get it cut?

4. Have you ever gotten a manicure? Why or why not?

5. Do you like tattoos? Why or why not?

6. Would you ever get your ears pierced? Why or why not?

> So, what color are you going to dye your hair?

> I think I'll go with blue and white, our school colors!

3 LISTENING

A **Use background knowledge.** Discuss the questions with a partner.

1. Do you think this is an attractive photo?

2. Do you take a lot of selfies? Why or why not?

B 🔊 **Listen for specific information.** You are going to hear an interview and complete an outline. Listen and complete the title for the outline below. **CD 1 Track 22**

Title: _____ to _____ the

_____ Selfie

I. ___*Before*___ you _____ the photo

   A. _____ different _____ in front of the _____

      1. see which ones look best

   B. neaten up your appearance

      1. _____ your hair

      2. check your _____

      3. wear _____ _____ to stand out

   C. take a selfie to _____ off something _____

      1. just gotten a _____

      2. _____ your _____ done

II. As the _____ is being taken

   A. consider the _____

      1. you want a _____ scene

   B. _____ the camera a bit

   C. watch out for _*photobombers*_

   D. _____ take a photo alone

      1. it's more fun with _____

C 🔊 **Listen for details; Take notes.** Listen and complete the rest of the outline. **CD 1 Track 23**

D 🔄 Strike your typical selfie pose. What face would you make to photobomb someone's picture? Show a partner.

> **Word Bank**
>
> *neaten up* = make neat; clean up
>
> *stand out* = be noticed
>
> *strike a pose* = get in position for a photo

WORLD LINK

Find a selfie online that you like and bring it to class. Who took the picture and where are they? What do you like about it?

4 SPEAKING

A 🔊 Listen to and read Chris and Tyler's conversation. Why does Chris want a tattoo? How does he feel and why does he feel that way? How does Tyler feel? **CD 1 Track 24**

CHRIS: Guess what? I'm getting a tattoo... right here on my right arm!

TYLER: Really? Are you sure?

CHRIS: Yeah. My best friend has one. It's really cool. Now I want one.

TYLER: But what do your parents think? Did they say anything?

CHRIS: They're not too happy... but I know it's going to look great!

TYLER: I see what you're saying, but...

CHRIS: And I found a really good tattoo artist.

TYLER: But what about the cost? Isn't it expensive?

CHRIS: No, it's not too bad—and I can pay half now and the rest later.

TYLER: Yeah, but what if you don't like it?

CHRIS: Don't worry.... It's going to look great!

B 🔁 Brainstorm reasons for and against getting a tattoo. Then practice the conversation with a partner.

SPEAKING STRATEGY

Useful Expressions: Disagreeing politely	
I agree up to a point.	I'm not sure it's / that's (such) a good idea. Are you sure?
Yes, but... / I know, but...	I see what you're saying, but...
I'm not sure. / I don't know.	I see what you mean, but...
But what about...?	I see where you're coming from, but...

C 🔁 Student A is planning to make a change in his or her appearance. Choose one of the ideas below (or one of your own). Role-play the situation. Then switch roles.

Student A: Tell your partner about your change. Give reasons why you want to do it.

Student B: Listen to your partner. Politely disagree. Use the Useful Expressions to help you.

shave your head

dye your hair

get your ears pierced

get plastic surgery

> Guess what? I'm getting my ears pierced.

> Really?

> Yeah. I think it'll look cool.

> But what about your parents? What are they going to say?

5 GRAMMAR

A Turn to page 199. Complete the exercises. Then do **B–D** below.

Adverbs Used with the Present Perfect			
	With questions	**With affirmative verbs**	**With negative verbs**
ever	Have you **ever** worn makeup?		I haven't **ever** worn makeup.
never		I've **never** worn makeup (before).	
yet	Have you taken a shower **yet**?		I haven't taken a shower **yet**.
still			I **still** haven't taken a shower.
already	Have you **already** taken a shower? Have you taken a shower **already**?	I've **already** taken a shower. I've taken a shower **already**.	
just		I've **just** finished shaving.	

B Arisa is planning her wedding. Read her comments below. Add the adverbs in parentheses to the correct place in the sentences.

Many people spend ten hours or more a week planning their wedding!

1. (ever) Wedding planning is difficult because I haven't done it before.

2. (already) We've made the guest list.

3. (yet) We haven't sent out the invitations.

4. (still) I haven't bought my wedding dress.

5. (never) I've hired a photographer before. I'm not sure what to do.

6. (just) We've booked the venue.

C Imagine you are planning a party for your friends. Add one of your own ideas to the checklist below. Then check (✓) off four things you have already done.

☐ decide on the menu ☐ make a guest list

☐ buy the food ☐ send out invitations

☐ choose a venue ☐ decorate the room

☐ come up with a playlist ☐ other_____

D 🔁 Work with a partner. Ask and answer questions about your party planning.

> I've decided on the menu, but I still haven't bought any food for the party.

> Have you chosen a venue yet?

> Not yet. But I'm thinking of holding the party outside.

6 COMMUNICATION

A Read the statements. Check (✓) if you *agree*, *disagree*, or are *not sure*.

Statements about men and women	agree	disagree	not sure
1. Older men and women shouldn't wear bright colors.			
2. For a woman, how much money a man has is more important than his looks.			
3. Men should never wear makeup.			
4. Women shouldn't get tattoos.			
5. Men worry about their appearance as much as women do.			
6. Women should always wear a skirt in formal settings.			
7. Men are first attracted to women because of their appearance.			
8. Athletic women are not attractive to men.			

B 🔵 Work with three other students. Compare and explain your answers from **A**. If one or more group members disagreed or was not sure, check (✓) the box of that item below.

1. ☐   5. ☐
2. ☐   6. ☐
3. ☐   7. ☐
4. ☐   8. ☐

> I checked *agree* for number 1. I just don't think older people look good in bright colors.

> I see what you're saying, but I also think they should wear whatever colors they want. I checked *disagree*.

C 🔵 As a group, work on each statement you checked in **B**. Rewrite the statement so that *everyone* agrees with it.

D 🔵 Present your group's statements to the class.

What kind of clothing do you think a person should wear to an event like this? Is it different or the same for men and women?

1 VOCABULARY

A 🔁 Take turns reading the story below aloud with a partner. Then match each two-word verb in blue with its definition (1–10).

1. _____ had a good relationship
2. _____ rejected, said *no* to an invitation
3. _*asked out*_ invited someone on a date
4. _____ end a romantic relationship
5. _____ became an adult

6. _____ stop thinking about someone
7. _____ go on a date
8. _____ met unexpectedly
9. _____ secretly dated another person
10. _____ started a machine

Alex liked Erin. One day he asked her out on a date. Erin was shy. At first she turned Alex down.

Alex asked Erin again, and she said *yes*. She agreed to go out with him.

They enjoyed spending time together. They got along well.

Unfortunately, Alex cheated on Erin. She saw him with another girl.

Erin was very upset. She decided to break up with Alex. They stopped dating.

Alex couldn't stop thinking about Erin. He couldn't get over her.

Erin and Alex grew up and got jobs: Erin worked as a banker, and Alex was a news reporter.

They lived in the same city but never ran into each other.

One day Erin turned on the TV and saw Alex. She decided to call him...

B 🔁 Work with a partner. Cover the sentences under the pictures. Take turns retelling Alex and Erin's story using the verbs in **A**.

C 🔁 What do you think happens next in their story? Tell a partner.

2 LISTENING

A 🔊 **Understand relationships.** Alex and Karen are talking about Gabe. Listen and write down the relationships. Use the words in the box. One word is extra. **CD 1 Track 25**

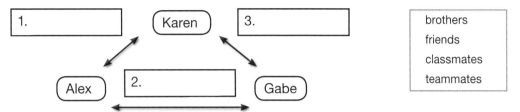

1. _____	Karen	3. _____
Alex	2. _____	Gabe

brothers
friends
classmates
teammates

B 🔊 **Complete a chart; Listen for details.** Listen. Complete the flow chart with the missing words. **CD 1 Track 26**

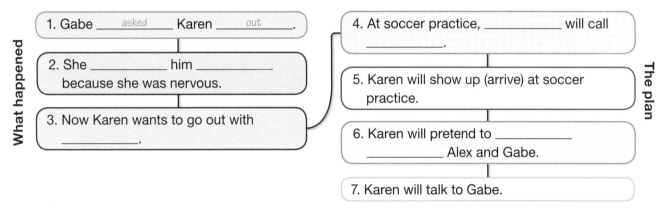

What happened

1. Gabe ___asked___ Karen ___out___.

2. She _____ him _____ because she was nervous.

3. Now Karen wants to go out with _____.

The plan

4. At soccer practice, _____ will call _____.

5. Karen will show up (arrive) at soccer practice.

6. Karen will pretend to _____ _____ Alex and Gabe.

7. Karen will talk to Gabe.

C 🔄 Try to answer the questions with a partner. Don't look back at your answers in **A** and **B**.

1. How do Alex, Karen, and Gabe know each other?

2. What happened to Karen?

3. What is her plan now? Do you think it will work? Why or why not?

D 🔗 You want to ask someone out on a date, but you're too shy. What do you do? Think of one or two ideas. Then get in a group and follow the directions below.

Speaker: Tell the group your ideas in **D**.

Listeners: For each idea a person says, use a sentence (a or b) to explain what you think.

a. The person may agree to go out with you because...

b. The person might turn you down because...

3 READING

A  **Use background knowledge.**
Answer the questions about dating.
Share your answers with a partner.

1. Where is the best place to meet
   someone?

   ☐ at school   ☐ at a party

   ☐ your idea: _____

2. What is the best way to meet
   someone?

   ☐ have a friend introduce you

   ☐ wait to be approached by the
   person

   ☐ your idea: _____

B **Read for details.** Read each person's
response to **Question 1** in the reading.
Did he or she go out on a date?
Check (✓) *Yes*, *No*, or *NM* (not
mentioned).

	Yes	No	NM
1. Mahesh			
2. Nina			
3. Kaleo			
4. Fumiko			

C **Infer information.** Read the responses
to **Question 2**. Which person do
you think would say each statement
below? Write his or her name. There is
one extra statement.

1. I can be shy, so dating one-on-one
   is hard. _____

2. I'm more of a dreamer than a
   realist. _____

3. I don't think looks are the most
   important thing. _____

4. I'm open to meeting someone my
   mom and dad know. _____

5. I want to meet someone who enjoys
   what I like to do. _____

D  Would you try any of the dating
methods mentioned? Why or why not?
Tell a partner.

A couple embraces in the
city center of Rome, Italy.

DATING AROUND THE WORLD

Do you want to go on a date? Are you still single? So are these people! We asked them two questions:

Question 1: **How did you recently meet someone?**

Mahesh: I went to an event recently in London. There is a long table. Guys sit on one side, and girls sit on the other. You talk to the person sitting across from you for three minutes, and then you move on to the next person. At the end of the evening, you choose the people you like. You're matched with the people that choose you, too... and then you go on dates with your matches!

Nina: I ran into this guy I knew from my college days. We went out on a couple of dates. He was nice. We had good conversation and got along OK, but there was no romantic spark.

Kaleo: I met a woman at work. I asked her out, but she turned me down. My friend says it's not good to date people you work with. I think he's probably right.

Fumiko: I went on an online dating site and talked to a few guys. I even went out with one of them and it was OK, but he was different than he was in his profile. I tried to meet more guys, but just looking at pictures and reading about people doesn't seem very romantic.

Question 2: **How would you like to meet someone?**

Mahesh: My parents are more traditional. They want to introduce me to a nice girl. When I was younger, I didn't like the idea. Now I think I might give it a try.

Nina: It's more relaxing to go out in a big group. I want to meet someone when I'm out with a group of friends. That feels more natural and not so stressful.

Kaleo: I love waterskiing and surfing. I heard that Internet dating is fun. You can read all about the other people and their interests before you contact them. That might work for me.

Fumiko: I'd like to meet someone in a romantic way. Imagine this: there is a huge rainstorm. A handsome stranger shares his umbrella with you. You and he fall in love. I know it sounds crazy, but that's my fantasy.

4 GRAMMAR

A Turn to page 200. Complete the exercises. Then do **B–D** below.

Phrasal Verbs	
Separable phrasal verbs	Please **turn on** <u>the TV</u>. Please **turn** <u>the TV</u> / <u>it</u> **on**. ~~Please **turn on** it.~~
Inseparable phrasal verbs	Erin **ran into** <u>Alex</u> / <u>him</u> yesterday.
Asking questions	Did he **ask** you **out**? When did they **break up**?

B 🔊 **Pronunciation: Coarticulation.** Read the information. Then listen and say the phrasal verbs. Draw a link to connect the words. **CD 1 Track 28**

> In each phrasal verb below, the verb ends in a consonant sound. The second word starts with a vowel. In spoken English, these two sounds link together, and the two words sound like one word.

1. ask out
2. break up
3. cheat on
4. give up
5. get along
6. get over
7. run into
8. turn on
9. make up

C 🔊 **Pronunciation: Coarticulation.** Listen to and repeat the sentences. Notice how different words link together. **CD 1 Track 29**

1. Alex cheated on Erin.
2. Turn on a light, please.
3. Don't worry. You'll get over it.
4. He asked her out.

D 👥 Work in a small group. Follow the steps below.

1. On nine small pieces of paper, write the numbers 1–9. Put them face down on the desk.

2. Take turns. Pick a number. Make a sentence or question using the phrasal verb from **B** that matches that number. Then put the number back. If you make a correct sentence or question, you get a point. <u>Do not use example sentences from this page</u>.

3. Play for 15 minutes. Who got the most points?

4. Repeat steps 1–3 with a new group and play again.

5 WRITING

A Read the short summary of Alex and Erin's story from page 56. What do you think happened next to the couple? Write another paragraph telling their story. Use at least three phrasal verbs from this lesson.

Alex and Erin: The Story Continues

Alex and Erin were high school sweethearts, but Alex cheated on Erin, and the couple broke up. Their story didn't end there, though. After high school, Erin went to college and later got a job in banking in a large city. Alex went to a different school, and in time, he became a news reporter in the same large city as Erin. The pair lived separate lives and never ran into each other. Then one day, Erin turned on the TV and saw Alex on the local news. "He's still so handsome," she thought, "but has he changed?" Erin decided to call him…

B Exchange papers with a partner.

1. Circle mistakes in your partner's story. Does your partner's story end happily?

2. Return the paper to your partner. Make corrections to your own story.

3. Read your final story to a new partner.

6 COMMUNICATION

A Complete the dating survey. Then write one question of your own about dating.

Dating Survey

1. What *first* attracts you to a person?
   a. looks
   b. personality
   c. intelligence
   d. common interests
   e. your idea: _____

2. Your boyfriend or girlfriend has cheated on you. What do you do?
   a. break up
   b. ignore it
   c. talk to him or her and make up
   d. wait for him or her to talk to me
   e. your idea: _____

3. What should you definitely do on a first date?
   a. bring a gift
   b. talk a lot
   c. offer to split the bill
   d. have *an exit plan* (a way to escape if the date is boring)
   e. your idea: _____

4. How would you break up with someone?
   a. over the telephone
   b. by email or text
   c. face-to-face
   d. by ignoring the person
   e. your idea: _____

5. Which is the *worst* dating situation?
   a. Your date arrives an hour late.
   b. Your date runs into an old girlfriend or boyfriend.
   c. Your date doesn't have enough money.
   d. Your date doesn't dress well.
   e. your idea: _____

6. Your question: _____
   _____

B Work in a small group. Take turns explaining your answers to each question in **A**. At the end, ask your question.

Would you like to go on a date in a place like this?

5 ACROSS CULTURES

Look at the photo. Answer the questions.

1 What custom is being shown in the photo?

2 When visitors come to your home, what do you customarily do?

3 What's an important custom in your country that visitors should know about?

UNIT GOALS

1 Describe good and bad behavior

2 Ask about culturally appropriate behavior

3 Compare customs in your country with those in other countries

4 Give advice on traveling abroad

Welcoming guests with a cup of tea is a custom in Turkey.

People use their phones to take pictures outside of a movie premier.

1 VIDEO Smartphone Addiction

A How much time do you spend on your phone every day? Discuss with a partner.

B Read the sentences and guess the missing words. Then watch and check your answers. The three people say they are *addicted* to their smartphones. What do you think that means?

1. "The first thing I do when I _____ up is grab for my phone."

2. Thirty-two-year-old Matthew Barrett is never _____ from his smartphone.

3. Matthew isn't the only one living his life almost completely _____.

4. "If I don't have my phone, I can't really do _____."

5. "I can't really go a _____ without it."

C Watch again. What do the experts say about smartphone addiction? Circle *True* or *False*.

1. Psychologists say smartphone users are dangerous.	True	False
2. As we connect more on our phones, we connect more in person.	True	False
3. Smartphone withdrawal can also cause physical problems.	True	False

D Discuss these questions with a partner.

1. What do you think of smartphone addiction? Do you agree with the experts?

2. When is it impolite or inappropriate to be on your smartphone?

2 VOCABULARY

In most cultures, being respectful and considerate to one's elders is expected.

A 🔁 Read sentences 1–8. Pay attention to the words in **blue**. What does each word mean? Tell a partner.

1. You should always be **pleasant** to other people, even when you're angry about something.

2. There are some situations when it's OK to be **impolite**.

3. An **honest** person always succeeds in the end. Tell the truth and you will, too.

4. It's not always easy to tell when someone is being **insincere**.

5. Being **disrespectful** is the worst thing you can do to your grandparents.

6. When you have a disagreement, the **mature** thing to do is walk away.

7. You should always be **considerate** of other people's feelings, even when they don't think about yours.

8. It's always **appropriate** to ask a question if you don't understand something.

Word Bank
Opposites
appropriate ↔ inappropriate
considerate ↔ inconsiderate
honest ↔ dishonest
kind ↔ unkind
mature ↔ immature
pleasant ↔ unpleasant
polite ↔ impolite / rude
respectful ↔ disrespectful
responsible ↔ irresponsible
sincere ↔ insincere

B Do you agree or disagree with the opinions in **A**? Write *A* or *D* next to each one.

C 🔁 Explain your answers in **B** to your partner.

> I agree that it's important to be respectful to other people.

3 LISTENING

A 🔄 **Build background knowledge.** Think of a school field trip you went on. Where did you go? What is one thing you were not allowed to do on the trip? Tell a partner.

B 🔊 **Listen for gist.** Listen. Complete the sentences.
CD 1 Track 30

1. The speaker is talking to a group of _____.

2. They are at a _____.

C **Make predictions.** Look at your answer for number 2 in **B**. This place has many different rules that visitors must follow. Can you guess what some of these rules are? Write them on a piece of paper.

D 🔊 **Check predictions; Listen to paraphrase.** Read the sentences. Then listen to the rules. Choose the best paraphrase for each rule that you hear. **CD 1 Track 31**

1. a. You must stay on the green and red paths.
   b. Always stay on the red path. You can leave the green path.

2. a. You cannot watch the staff feeding the animals.
   b. Feeding time is open to the public.

3. a. Running or making noise is not allowed anywhere.
   b. Running or making noise is only permitted in certain areas.

4. a. Birds walk freely around some areas. Please don't touch them.
   b. Birds walk freely around some areas. It's OK to touch them.

5. a. You're not allowed to eat lunch inside this place.
   b. You can enjoy lunch inside this place.

6. a. If you don't know what's recyclable, just ask.
   b. Everything goes into the recycling containers.

E 🔄 Would you like to visit this place? Why or why not? Tell a partner.

F 🔊 **Pronunciation: Linking the same sounds.** Listen and repeat the words. **CD 1 Track 32**

1. don't touch   2. want to   3. steak came   4. left twenty   5. all loved   6. Tom might

G 🔄 **Pronunciation: Linking the same sounds.** With a partner, take turns reading aloud about Mari's dinner. Notice the underlined consonant sounds.

> Tom, Sue, and I had dinner together. The waiter was polite and considerate. I had the most delicious soup. Tom's steak came out quickly, and it was perfectly cooked. We all loved the place. We left twenty dollars for a tip. I would definitely eat there again. In fact, Tom might go there again tonight!

ℹ️ Say each pair of underlined consonants as one long sound. You don't need to say each sound twice.

H 🔊 🔄 **Pronunciation: Linking the same sounds.** Now listen to the story in **G** and practice saying it with a partner. Pay attention to the linked consonant sounds. **CD 1 Track 33**

4 SPEAKING

A 🔊 Read and listen to Ahmed and Inez's conversation. Why are people going to Ahmed's house? What custom is Inez unsure about? **CD 1 Track 34**

INEZ: Wow! Everything smells delicious, Ahmed. How long did it take you to cook all this?

AHMED: A few hours. But don't worry—I like to cook for my friends. And I like to have dinner parties. Please, sit down.

INEZ: Um, can I sit anywhere?

AHMED: Sure. You're the first guest to arrive. Make yourself comfortable.

INEZ: You know, I've never had Turkish food before.

AHMED: Don't worry. I'll explain everything... Uh, here, try this.

INEZ: Um, is it OK if I use my fingers?

AHMED: Sure, go right ahead. So, what do you think?

INEZ: Mmm. It's delicious.

B 🔁 Practice the conversation with a partner.

SPEAKING STRATEGY

C Read the Useful Expressions. Which responses are positive? Which are negative?

Useful Expressions: Asking about culturally appropriate behavior	

Is it OK / appropriate to use my fingers?
Is it OK if I use my fingers?
  Please, go right ahead. / Absolutely.
  Actually, it's probably better to use a fork.
  Normally, people use a fork.
	Is it all right to wear shoes inside?
	Is it all right if I wear shoes inside?
	  Sure, no problem. / Yeah, it's fine.
	  Actually, it's best to remove your shoes.
	  No, you really should take off your shoes.

D 🔁 Read the rules for the two situations below. Role-play one of the situations with a partner. One person asks about the culturally appropriate behavior. The other explains them. Then switch roles and role-play another situation.

Rules for visiting a mosque	
wear shoes inside	☹
wear shorts	☹
cover your head	☺
sit in a mixed group of men and women	☹

Rules for a formal Japanese dinner	
help yourself to a drink	☹
make special food requests	☹
ask for a knife and fork	☺
leave a tip	☹

Is it appropriate to ask for a knife and fork? I can't use chopsticks.

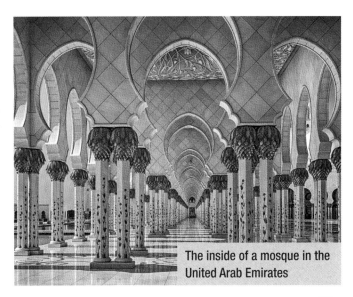

The inside of a mosque in the United Arab Emirates

5 GRAMMAR

A Turn to page 201. Complete the exercises. Then do **B–D** below.

It + be + Adjective + Infinitive; Gerund + be + Adjective						
It	*be*	**Adjective**	*(for)*	**(pronoun)**	**Infinitive**	
It	**was**(n't)	hard	(for)	(me)	to pass	the test.
It's (not)		normal	(for)	(us)	to eat	with chopsticks.
Gerund			*be*	**Adjective**	*(for)*	**(pronoun)**
Passing	the test		**was**(n't)	hard	(for)	(me).
Eating	with chopsticks		**is**(n't)	normal	(for)	(us).

B Use the key words to write two sentences about learning English.

1. English / study / fun

It's fun

Studying

2. impossible / master / for anyone / English grammar

3. for language students / English / speak / unnecessary / perfectly

4. practice conversation with / important / a native speaker / find

C 🔁 Look at the statements in **B**. Do you agree or disagree with each one? Discuss your answers with a partner.

> I think studying English is sometimes fun.

> Really? It's never fun for me!

D 🔁 What would you do in these situations? Discuss your ideas with a partner.

1. There is an empty seat next to you on the train. Is it OK to put your bag there? Why or why not?

2. You are in a crowded elevator, and your phone rings. Is it OK to answer the call? Why or why not?

> I think it's inconsiderate for you to put your bag on the seat. It takes up too much space.

> It depends. If the train is mostly empty, putting your bag on the seat seems appropriate.

6 COMMUNICATION

A Study the people in the subway scene below. What are they doing? Use the words in the box and make sentences about their behavior. Share them with a partner.

> One woman is eating ice cream on the subway. I think it's inappropriate because...

(im)polite	(in)appropriate	(in)considerate	(un)kind

B You are going to design a poster. Read the information below and look at the examples. Work as a group to plan your poster. Then draw it on a piece of paper.

- The city is starting a public awareness campaign for buses and subways.
- Officials are asking riders to design a poster for the campaign.
- The winners will each receive a free one-year bus and subway pass!

C Put up your posters around the room. Vote for the best one.

Giving up your seat on the subway is the polite thing to do!

MTSDC

Hey, you! Slow down!
I know you're in a hurry but...

Remember! Running in the subway station is dangerous. It can result in serious injury.

MTSDC

Body language can be an important way of communicating with other people.

1 VOCABULARY

A Match the words in groups A and B to make common English expressions. Then match the expressions to their definitions below. Use the underlined words as clues to help you.

A				B			
body	eye	jet	personal	~~barrier~~	expression	~~lag~~	space
eating	facial	~~language~~	~~small~~	contact	habits	language	talk

1. <u>words</u> that <u>prevent you from understanding</u> another person   <u>language</u>   <u>barrier</u>
2. feeling <u>tired</u> after a long <u>airplane</u> trip   _____   <u>lag</u>
3. describing <u>how or when</u> people <u>eat</u>   _____   _____
4. the <u>look</u> on a person's <u>face</u> (for example, a smile)   _____   _____
5. <u>conversation</u> about <u>unimportant or everyday</u> things   <u>small</u>   _____
6. <u>looking directly at</u> another person's <u>eyes</u>   _____   _____
7. the <u>area</u> around each <u>person</u>   _____   _____
8. <u>communication</u> through how we move our <u>bodies</u>   _____   _____

B Think of a country you would like to visit. Imagine you are going there for three months. Complete the questionnaire on the top of the next page. Write your answers on a separate piece of paper.

A country I want to visit: _____

Arrival

1. Will you have jet lag at the start of your visit? If yes, how can you avoid it?

Communication

2. Will there be a language barrier, or will it be easy to communicate with others?

Food

3. Are the eating habits in this country similar to yours? Why or why not?

Body language

4. Is it OK to make eye contact with people? Is it OK to stand close to others?

<table>
<tr><td>**Word Bank**</td></tr>
<tr><td>**Word Partnerships**
have ↔ *avoid* jet lag
make eye contact / small talk
overcome a language barrier</td></tr>
</table>

C 🔁 Share your ideas in **B** with a partner. Do you think it will be easy to adjust to your host country? Why or why not?

2 LISTENING

A 🔊 **Listen for gist.** You will hear three selections from different lectures. What is each lecture about? Listen and write the correct answer (a–e) below. Two topics are extra. **CD 1 Track 35**

| a. body language   b. eating habits   c. eye contact   d. personal space   e. small talk |

Lecture #1: _____   Lecture #2: _____   Lecture #3: _____

B 🔊 **Take notes on key details.** Before you listen, write in the topic (from **A**) for each lecture. Then listen and complete the notes below. Write only one or two words per blank. **CD 1 Track 35**

Lecture #1: _____

  I. Conversations about _____ things

  II. Popular topics:

      1. _____

      2. _____

      3. _shared experiences_

Lecture #2: _____

  I. You can understand a person just by _____ him or her.

    1. Communication:

      a. _____ %: the words we use

      b. _____ %: the way our _____

Lecture #3: _____

  I. How to make a good _____

    1. DO

      a. _____ at the person

    2. DON'T

      a. _____ at someone because the person will feel _____

C 🔁 Think about the topics of the three lectures. Pick one lecture and think of a time when you either used or saw something from the lecture in real life. Tell a partner about your experience.

3 READING

WELCOME TO **BOGOTÁ**

A 🔁 **Use background knowledge.** Read the title of the article. What do you know about this city or the country it's in? Tell a partner.

B **Understand purpose.** Read the passage. Then complete the sentence below.

The main purpose of this reading is to _____ in Bogotá.

a. teach tourists about famous sites

b. help foreign students adjust to life

c. explain how to do business

C Complete the sentences with the words from the article.

exhausted	cues
presentable	discouraged

1. I didn't sleep on the flight, so I was _____ when we landed.

2. I watched for _____ from my friend, so I knew how to act around his family.

3. She didn't get _____ when she did poorly on the test. She studied harder and did well on the next one.

4. It is important to be _____. You should dress well in public.

D 🔁 What would be the hardest thing for you to adjust to in Bogotá? Tell a partner.

WORLD LINK

Research another city. Write tips like the ones in the article about this city. Share your tips with the class.

Bogotá, Colombia, is a well-known city. Every year, thousands of students from all over the world visit it to learn Spanish and travel to other places around Colombia. Now that you've arrived, here are some things to keep in mind.

1. **Jet lag.** If you traveled a long way, you'll probably be exhausted for the first few days. When you feel sleepy, the best thing to do is stay awake. If you fall asleep during the day, you'll wake up at night, and it will take days to get on a normal schedule!

2. **Greeting people.** When you meet people, it's polite to make eye contact. Many people will also make small talk. Be ready to talk about your health, your family, and of course, your trip! Another thing to keep in mind is that people in many parts of Colombia can be more reserved than in other Latin American countries. You should always start off a conversation by being very respectful. From there, you can follow the cues[1] of the other people in the conversation.

3. **Learning the language.** Learning a new language is hard, and being frustrated is part of the process. But don't get discouraged! Pay attention to body language, facial expressions, gestures, and context, and your language abilities will get stronger over time. Colombia is one of the fastest-growing countries for students

from other countries who want to learn Spanish. There are a large number of language schools and private teachers to help you.

4. **Lifestyle changes.** As you start to make new friends here, you'll notice people are very active. When people go out, dancing is very popular. You should learn how to do it. Smoking is uncommon, and it is illegal to do it in public places. Finally, it's important to look presentable in public at all times, so don't wear sweatpants if you're going out. This is a great place to break some of your bad habits and get healthier!

5. **Homesickness.** You will miss your home, family, and friends. This might make you feel sad, which is completely normal. To feel better, try keeping a few things from home around, like pictures or a favorite food. Don't overdo it, though. You should also connect to your new city. Go sightseeing with a classmate, or try new activities, like playing a sport. The more you socialize, the better you'll feel.

Most of all, remember that studying abroad is a life-changing event. You're going to learn a lot about a new country and about yourself, too. All of this takes time, but in the end, you will make friends and memories that will last for many years!

[1]If you follow someone else's *cue*, you copy their behavior.

4 GRAMMAR

A Turn to page 202. Complete the exercises. Then do **B** and **C** below.

Present and Future Time Clauses with *before, after, when, as soon as / once*	
Main clause	**Time clause**
In Spain, people often <u>kiss</u> each other	**when** they <u>meet</u>.
Please <u>remove</u> your shoes	**before** you <u>enter</u> the temple.
<u>We're going to go</u> to the park	**after** we <u>eat</u> lunch.
<u>I'll call</u> you	**as soon as** / **once** we <u>arrive</u>.
Time clause	**Main clause**
Before you enter the temple,	please remove your shoes.

B Read about the four people's problems living abroad. What should each person do? Match each person with a piece of advice (a–h).

a. Skype your family.

b. Watch TV shows with subtitles.

c. Take a cooking class.

d. Spend time with friends.

e. Join a club.

f. Ask your teacher or host family for help.

g. Go on a short trip.

h. My idea: _____

"At home I'm very outgoing, but I don't know anyone here, so I'm kind of shy."

—Jin Soo in Europe

"People here are nice, but I'm homesick. I want to quit school and go home."

—Clara in North America

"I feel discouraged. I studied before I came here, but I can't communicate with anyone very well. I want to improve my language skills."

—Julia in Africa

"I like the food here, but I can only order two or three dishes, so I'm always eating the same thing!"

—Yusef in Asia

C ⟳ Work with a partner. Follow the steps below.

1. **Student A:** Take the role of one person above. Explain your problem.

   Student B: Give the person some advice using *Before / When / After / As soon as / Once you...*

2. Change roles and repeat step 1.

3. Repeat steps 1 and 2.

> Clara, I know you're homesick. Before you quit and go home, spend time with friends here. Once you do this, maybe you'll feel better.

5 WRITING

How to Make Small Talk at a Party
(when you don't speak the language well)

1. Be prepared.
Before you go to the party, think of two or three things to talk about.
Popular topics: sports, music, things in the news

2. Ask a question.
Once you make eye contact with someone at the party, say *hi*, and introduce yourself.

Then ask a simple question to get the conversation started: *Where are you from?*

3. Keep things light.
After you start talking, remember to keep things light. It's easier to talk about simple topics.

A A student has prepared a short presentation. Read the slides and answer the questions with a partner.

1. What is the topic of his *how-to* presentation?

2. What are his three suggestions? Explain each in your own words.

3. Are these good ideas? Can you think of one more suggestion to add?

B Choose an idea from the list of travel topics and prepare a short presentation about it. Organize your presentation like the example, with a title and three tips. Remember to use time clauses.

> **Travel topics: How to...**
> - feel better when you're homesick.
> - pack for your trip.
> - overcome a language barrier.
> - stay safe when you travel.
> - my idea: _____

6 COMMUNICATION

A Work in a small group. Follow the directions. Repeat until each student has a chance to give his or her presentation.

Speaker: Give your presentation from Writing using your slides. Remember to explain the point on each slide in more detail. Use the language below to organize your talk.

Listeners: Answer questions 1–3 in **A** in Writing about the speaker's ideas.

> Today, I'm going to talk about how to make small talk. The first thing you should do is...

Word Bank
Explaining how to do something
Today, I'm going to talk about how to...
The first thing you should do is...
A second thing to do is...
And finally...
Thanks for listening. Do you have any questions?

6 BUSINESS AND MARKETING

Look at the photo. Answer the questions.

1 Where is this shopping district? What kinds of products are sold there?

2 How many advertisements do you see or hear every day? Where do you encounter them?

3 What is one advertisement that is popular now in your country?

UNIT GOALS

1 Describe and ask questions about companies

2 Emphasize important points

3 Give an opinion about different advertisements

4 Review a product

Colorful billboards advertise video games and other computer goods in a popular shopping area in Tokyo.

Bottles of Sriracha sauce

1 VIDEO Sriracha

A Do you like spicy food? If so, what are your favorite dishes? If not, why not? Tell a partner.

B You are going to watch a video about spicy Sriracha sauce. Complete each sentence with a number from the box.

20	30	50	70	200,000
25	40	60	4,000	250,000

1. They make Sriracha sauce in a $ _____ million plant.

2. They produce _____ bottles of the sauce each day.

3. The main ingredient, jalapeno peppers, comes from a farm _____ miles away.

4. Farmer Craig Underwood has worked with David Tran for _____ years.

5. Tran started with just _____ acres (202,000 square meters) of land.

6. Next year he will have _____ acres (16.2 square kilometers).

7. There are more than _____ barrels in the warehouse.

8. Last year the company sold $ _____ million in sauce.

9. It's growing _____ % each year.

10. David Tran has worked on his product for more than _____ years.

C What is the most interesting or surprising thing about David's story? Tell a partner.

WORLD LINK

Go online and read more about Sriracha sauce. What new information did you learn? Report back to the class.

2 VOCABULARY

A Read the sentences. How many of the words in **blue** do you know? What do they mean? Use your dictionary to help you. Compare your answers with a partner's.

1. They plan to **advertise** their new product on TV and online.

2. If you **consume** too many calories, you'll gain weight.

3. Since our sales plan isn't working, we'll have to **develop** a new one.

4. Their company is pretty small. It only **employs** 20 people.

5. They are looking for someone to **invest** $2 million in the project.

6. Ms. Park is the head of that department. She **manages** ten people.

7. A: What does your company make?
   B: It **produces** batteries for phones.

8. My doctor **promotes** walking as a way to lose weight.

9. Do you want to buy something? To **purchase** an item, please click on the *Buy now* button.

10. Once we receive your money, we'll **ship** your order to you.

B Complete the chart with the noun forms of the verbs. Be careful of the spelling! Check your answers in a dictionary.

Nouns ending in *–ment*				Nouns ending in *–tion*	
advertise	advertisement	invest		consume	consumption
develop		manage		produce	
employ		ship		promote	

C Make four questions using the words in **A** and **B**. Take turns asking the questions with a partner.

What have you purchased online recently?

I downloaded a couple of songs from iTunes.

How many people does Samsung employ?

I don't know, but since it's a large international company it's probably a large number.

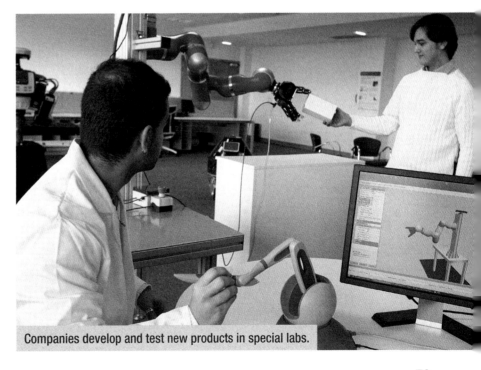

Companies develop and test new products in special labs.

3 LISTENING

A Circle the things that you do a lot. Where are you when you do these things?

send emails   watch videos   send text messages   talk on the phone

B 🔊 **Listen for the main idea.** Read the questions and responses below. Listen and circle the best answer to each question. **CD 1 Track 37**

1. What is the main purpose of the article Lian is reading?
   a. to talk about how many hours we spend online
   b. to describe our Internet habits
   c. to give tips for using the Internet well
   d. to give solutions for Internet addiction

2. What does the article say about the two groups of people?
   a. Everyone wants to stay connected.
   b. They both get specific information online.
   c. They go online for different reasons.
   d. The number of people in both groups is increasing.

C 🔊 🔄 Listen again. Describe Arturo's and Lian's online behavior with a partner. How are they different? **CD 1 Track 37**

D 🔊 **Listen for details; Identify a speaker.** What reasons does Arturo give to explain his behavior? Listen again and circle your answers. **CD 1 Track 37**

1. He doesn't like social media.
2. He likes to know what's new.
3. He only goes online for specific reasons.
4. He wants to stay connected.

E 🔄 Are you more like Arturo or Lian? How so? Discuss with a partner.

F 🔊 **Pronunciation: Stress on nouns and verbs with the same spelling.** Listen and repeat the following sentences. Note where the stress falls in the underlined words. **CD 1 Track 38**

NOUN: How many <u>PRE</u>sents did you get for your birthday?

VERB: He pre<u>SENTS</u> his ideas to the board at 2:00.

G 🔊 Practice saying these sentences. Then listen and repeat. **CD 1 Track 39**

NOUN	VERB
1. a. What's your email <u>address</u>?	b. I need to <u>address</u> this package.
2. a. You should check the <u>record</u>.	b. You should try <u>recording</u> your hours.
3. a. There has been an <u>increase</u> in numbers.	b. The number of users is <u>increasing</u>.

4 SPEAKING

A 🔊 Complete the interview by filling in the missing questions. Write the correct numbers in the blanks. Then listen and check your answers.
CD 1 Track 40

1. Can I get one of your audiobooks?
2. How exactly do you do that—put people first?
3. Maybe you've seen one of our advertisements online?
4. So, my first question is, what *does* Sound Smart do exactly?
5. What is the main focus of your company?
6. Where can I get an application?

HOST: I'd like to welcome Beverly Smith, the CEO for Sound Smart Inc., to our show today. Welcome, Beverly! _____

BEVERLY: Well, as you know, a lot of people are studying English. And many of them want to be able to study anywhere, so we produce audiobooks... _____

HOST: Yes, I have. What a great idea—how convenient! _____

BEVERLY: Sure. After you make a purchase, you can download the book online. It's simple.

HOST: _____

BEVERLY: Well, we really believe in our employees. The bottom line is that happy employees make a good product. So our company slogan is *People First!*

HOST: _____

BEVERLY: Well, for one thing, we have a lot of perks.* Our company has its own gym in the building. Also, each of our 100 employees gets the day off on his or her birthday.

HOST: Nice! _____

*perks = extra things you receive because of your job (for example, extra holidays, etc.)

B 🔄 Now cover the conversation in **A** and complete the company profile of Sound Smart with a partner.

Name of company: *Sound Smart*

Product / Service: _____

Company slogan: _____

Perks: _____

Other: _____

Useful Expressions
Asking about companies
What does your company do exactly?
What is the main focus of your company?
How do you...?
Emphasizing important points
I'd like to emphasize that...
Never forget that...
This is a key point.
The bottom line is...

SPEAKING STRATEGY

C 🔄 Work with a partner to create your own company. On a piece of paper, make a company profile.

D 🔄 You're going to tell another pair of students about your company. Prepare a short presentation with your partner. Use the Useful Expressions to help you emphasize certain points.

E 👥 Take turns presenting to another pair. The students who are listening should ask questions similar to those in **A**. Would you like to work for the company you heard about? Why or why not?

5 GRAMMAR

A Turn to page 203. Complete the exercises. Then do **B–D** below.

The Passive Voice: Simple Present and Simple Past			
Subject	***be* + past participle**	***by* + object**	**Questions**
Audiobooks	**are made**	**by** Sound Smart.	Are audiobooks made by Sound Smart?
The company	**was founded**	**by** Beverly Smith.	How are the books made?

B Read these sentences about a neighborhood. Then rewrite each sentence as a passive sentence. Include the object where needed.

1. People settled this neighborhood 200 years ago.
   This neighborhood was
   _____

2. Everyone knows the neighborhood for its cute shops and boutiques.
   _____

3. They call the main shopping street Hoyt Street.
   _____

4. Merchants sell clothing and household goods.
   _____

5. The residents use many different forms of transportation to get around.
   _____

6. Some neighbors hold street fairs in the summer.
   _____

C 🔁 In which passive sentences in **B** did you include the object (*by* + noun)? Why did you leave the object out of the other sentences? Tell a partner.

D 🔁 Write questions in the passive for the statements in **B**. Then ask a partner those questions about his or her own neighborhood.

> When was your neighborhood settled?

> I'm not sure exactly, but I *do* know it's very old.

6 COMMUNICATION

A Look at the map and photos. Then read about Iceland and answer the four questions with a partner.

1. Is Iceland a big or small country?

2. Is it hot or cold there?

3. What else do you know about Iceland?

4. How is it different from your country?

B With a partner, state the different facts about Iceland. Use active and passive sentences. Use the verbs in the box in your description.

import / **export** (food, gas, products)
make / **produce** (cars, electronics)
find / **see** (natural wonders, wild animals)
grow (produce)
speak (languages)

> Many hot springs are found in Iceland.

> You can see polar bears there.

C With a partner, make a list of facts about your city, region, or country. Use at least three of the verbs from the box in **B**. Present your list of facts to the class.

Iceland

Population: 330,000

Capital city: Reykjavik

Literacy rate: Almost 100%

Natural wonders: Glaciers, geysers, waterfalls, hot springs

Government: Democracy (the world's oldest)

Animals: Cattle, sheep, polar bears, seabirds

Produce: Turnips, potatoes

Exports: Seafood

Money: Icelandic krona

Languages: Icelandic, English, Nordic languages

Activities: Whale watching, hiking, skiing

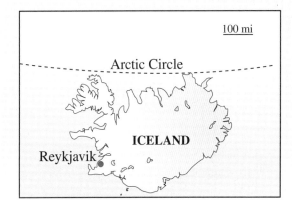

a glacier

a waterfall

LESSON B ADVERTISING

A man makes trades on the stock market.

1 VOCABULARY

A Study the graph at the right. Then read about the retail industry and answer the questions with a partner. Is most of the news positive or negative? How do you know? What is the positive news?

(a) Overall, the retail industry is **in a slump**. Experts expect the situation to **get worse** before the economy can **recover**. **Profits** continue to be **down**. **(b)** For the last few years, a number of companies have experienced a **sharp fall** in profits. Newspapers continue to struggle. **(c)** There has been a **steady decline** in in-store purchases for the third year in a row. But there is one bright spot in the news: **(d)** The number of retail companies advertising on the Internet has **increased dramatically**, and **(e)** overall consumer spending online has **risen slightly**.

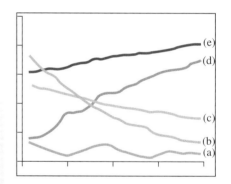

Word Bank
in a slump = a period when the economy is not doing well
profits = income; money earned

B Use some of the words in blue to complete the chart.

	Adjectives	Adverbs	Verbs / Nouns
small in amount	slight	_____	(↑) _____, _____
constant, not sudden	gradual, _____	gradually, steadily	(↓) decrease, _____,
large in amount, sudden	dramatic, _____	_____, sharply	_____

C 🔁 Read about the graphs. Then use the words in the box to complete sentences about them. You will use one of the words twice. Compare your answers with a partner's.

decrease	gradual	rose	a slump
down	increase	slightly	up

1. We've seen a(n) _____ _____ in unemployment, but numbers are still _____.

2. New car sales are in _____. Recently they _____ _____.

3. The number of students studying English is _____ and ___down___, but overall there has been a(n) _____.

2 LISTENING

A 🔁 What is a commercial that you can remember? What do you remember most about it (the words, a character, a song)? Tell a partner.

B 🔊 **Take notes; Listen for specific information.** Listen to three commercials. What kind of product is advertised in each one? Write down key words you hear. **CD 1 Track 41**

1. Product: _____

   Key words: _____

2. Product: _____

   Key words: _____

3. Product: _____

   Key words: _____

Word Bank
catchy = fun and easy to remember
clever = funny or interesting in a smart way
slogan = a short, easy-to-remember phrase used in an ad to sell a product

C 🔊 🔁 **Listen for gist.** Listen again. How did each ad try to make you buy the product? Circle the correct answer. Then explain your answers to a partner. **CD 1 Track 41**

Ad 1: a. It told a moving story.

   b. It made a personal connection.

Ad 2: a. It talked about an innovative product.

   b. It had a catchy slogan.

Ad 3: a. It targeted specific people.

   b. It had a jingle.

D 🔁 Would you buy or use any of these products? Discuss with a partner.

3 READING

A 🔁 Do you think advertising is necessary to sell products? Why or why not? Tell a partner.

B 🔁 **Identify a point of view; Draw conclusions.** Read the article. How would the author of the article answer the question in **A**? Use information from the article to explain your answer to a partner.

C **Scan for details.** Complete the sentences with the correct information.

1. Many people think that ads are a _____ influence.

2. The law in São Paulo took down over _____ billboards.

3. The ads in São Paulo covered _____ and _____ that needed to be cleaned.

4. The ads were replaced by _____.

5. One of the best ways to learn about new products is by _____ - _____ - _____, that is, from family and friends.

6. _____ reviews are a modern version of word-of-mouth.

D 🔁 Answer the questions with a partner.

1. Do you think it's a good idea to limit ads in public places, like they did in São Paulo?

2. Do you think that there are too many ads in your city?

3. Has an ad ever persuaded you to buy or do something?

4. Have you ever read online reviews of a product? Do you trust them? Why or why not?

Is advertising really necessary? Billions of dollars are spent on it every year, so it must be important. After all, it's a busy world. You have to advertise to get people's attention to sell products!

But there is a downside to this. Researchers say that ads can negatively influence people to make them feel like they should be someone else. They argue that the ads are deceptive[1] and create a false sense of reality. Research has even shown that many children can't tell the difference between an ad and real life!

Others believe there are too many ads and that they make cities look unattractive. Some cities are taking action. In 2006, a law was passed in São Paulo, Brazil, that prohibited ads such as outdoor posters and billboards.[2] Over 15,000 billboards were taken down. This has caused people to look at their city in a new way. Before, their attention was constantly drawn to the large number of ads on

the streets. But now, people are able to clearly view and enjoy the beauty of the old buildings and modern structures.

In addition, problems that existed in the city for years are now getting fixed. For example, some neighborhoods needed to be cleaned and buildings needed to be repaired, but ads covered those areas and made them easy to ignore. When the billboards came down, people noticed the problems and started to fix them. Now these buildings are covered in beautiful art. São Paulo was one of the first major cities to pass a law like this, but now other cities, such as Paris, Tehran, and New York, have taken steps to reduce the number of advertisements on the streets.

So, how do people hear about new products now? One of the oldest, and best, ways is still word-of-mouth. People trust friends, family, and people they talk to more than they trust billboards. This makes word-of-mouth very persuasive![3] Word-of-mouth advertising has other advantages, too. It's cost-effective (after all, it's free), and a company doesn't have to create a complex business plan to do it.

Many people also use the Internet to review and share products. This is similar to word-of-mouth because people discuss opinions and personal experiences, but many more people can be part of the conversation. You have to be careful about online reviews, though. Unlike a suggestion from a friend or family member, you don't always know who is posting a review online!

[1]If something is *deceptive*, it makes you believe something that is not true.
[2]A *billboard* is a large ad on a sign.
[3]If something is *persuasive*, it makes someone believe something.

4 GRAMMAR

A Turn to page 204. Complete the exercises. Then do **B** and **C** below.

Connecting Ideas with *because, so, although / even though*	
She uses that product **Because** it's the cheapest,	**because** it's the cheapest. she uses that product.
This snack is 100% natural,	**so** a lot of moms buy it for their kids.
Many people buy that car **Even though** / **Although** it's expensive,	**even though** / **although** it's expensive. many people buy that car.

B With a partner, combine the sentences using *because, so,* or *although / even though*.

1. Female models in clothing ads are very thin. Girls want to be very thin.

   _____

2. Lottery ads show people winning a lot of money. Most people don't win any money.

   _____

3. Energy drinks are advertised on sites popular with teens. Teens buy more of these drinks.

   _____

4. A TV ad shows only boys playing with a popular toy. Girls like the toy, too.

   _____

C Answer questions 1–4 below with a partner. Use *so, because, although,* and *even though* to explain your opinions.

Should…

1. very thin models be used in clothing ads for women?

2. lottery ads be shown on TV?

3. energy drinks be advertised on sites popular with teens?

4. some toys be advertised to boys (or girls) only?

> Even though it's important to look good, the girls in clothing ads are too thin. It's not healthy.

> I agree, so I don't shop at those stores.

5 WRITING

A Read the product review. Answer the questions with a partner.

1. What product is the person reviewing?

2. What are the good and bad things about it?

3. Does the person give the product a mostly positive or negative review?

B Think of something you bought recently. What are the positive and negative things about this product? Make notes. Then use your ideas and the example to help you write a product review.

THIS PRODUCT IS RATED: ★★★★★

I like to go mountain biking. When it's hot, I need to drink a lot of water. I like to use my Hydro-Pak because I can ride and drink at the same time! The Hydro-Pak is convenient and lightweight, and it comes in many different colors. Although it's more expensive than other models, it definitely is the best!

C ⟳ Exchange your writing with a partner. Read his or her review.

1. Are there any mistakes? If yes, circle them.

2. Answer the questions in **A** about your partner's product. Do you know this product? Do you agree with your partner's review?

3. Return the paper to your partner. Make corrections to your own review.

4. Publish a collection of class product reviews.

6 COMMUNICATION

The Citybike Mini:
"The Foldable Bike"

Pros: It's…
- lightweight.
- easy to store at school or work.
- easy to carry on public transportation.

Cons: It's…
- expensive.
- only good for short bike rides.

A ⟳ You and your partner work for an advertising agency. You need to create a minute-long commercial for TV or the Internet for the product above. On a piece of paper, write your ideas. As you create the ad, think about the questions below. Then practice doing your commercial.

1. Does the ad have a catchy slogan or song?

_____

2. Which word(s) best describe(s) the ad; circle your choice(s):

moving   clever   inspiring   other: _____

3. Is the ad persuasive? Would you buy the product after watching the ad? Why or why not?

_____

B ⚙ Get together with another pair and perform your commercial for them. When you watch, answer questions 1–3 in **A**. Then explain your answers to the presenters using *because*, *so*, and *even though / although.*

> Even though the ad was clever, I don't think people would buy the bike because…

1 STORYBOARD

A Al is always borrowing things from his friend Manny. Look at the pictures and complete the conversations. More than one answer is possible for each blank.

B 🔁 Practice the conversations with a partner. Then change roles and practice again.

2 SEE IT AND SAY IT

A 🔁 Look at the pictures of Julia and Dan and answer the questions. Use some of the verbs from the box in your answers. Work with a partner.

ask out	catch up	get along	go out	run into	work out

1. Where are Julia and Dan in each picture? What are they doing?
2. In the first picture, what do you think happened? What is Dan saying to Julia?
3. In the second situation, what do you think they are talking about?

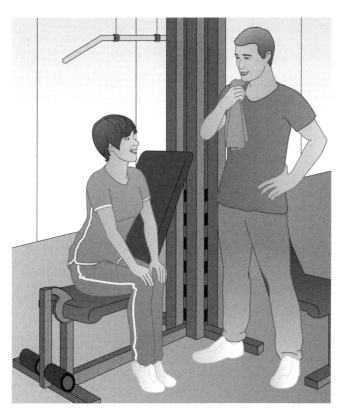 

B 🔁 Write a conversation for each situation on a separate piece of paper. Practice the conversations with your partner.

C 👥 Get together with another pair. Take turns acting out your conversations.

3 THE CULTURAL ICEBERG

A Read about the cultural iceberg and some information about Japan. Circle the correct answers.

Culture is similar to an iceberg. There are cultural rules that are visible and easy to understand. Most of our cultural values, however, are invisible or hidden. For example, when you visit a traditional restaurant in Japan, people may sit on the floor and use chopsticks to eat. These eating habits / facial expressions are easy to come across / figure out. You may not know, however, that while it's common / uncommon for men to sit cross-legged on the floor, it can be considered appropriate / inappropriate for women to do so. You have to study people's personal space / body language to understand this less visible cultural rule.

B Now think about your own country. Complete the chart with cultural *dos* and *don'ts* (the rules of behavior) that you think are important.

	Eating habits	Small talk	Body language
Dos			
Don'ts			

C Share your cultural *dos* and *don'ts* with a partner. Which idea is the most interesting? Share it with the class.

4 LISTENING

A You will hear a question or statement and three responses spoken in English. Select the best response to the question or statement and circle the letter (A, B, C). **CD 1 Track 43**

1. A   B   C   4. A   B   C

2. A   B   C   5. A   B   C

3. A   B   C   6. A   B   C

5 COMMUNICATION

A  Read the famous advertising slogans. Complete each one with a word from the box. Guess with a partner.

beautiful	different	dreams	driving	flowers	~~milk~~	skies	nothing

1. "Got _____milk_____?"

2. "Say it with _____."

3. "Fly the friendly _____."

4. "Think _____."

5. "The ultimate _____ machine."

6. "Impossible is _____."

7. "Easy, breezy, _____ CoverGirl."

8. "Where _____ come true."

B With a partner, look at the slogans in **A** again. Can you match each one to a company or brand below?

BMW

Adidas

California Milk Processor Board

Disney World

Florists' Transworld Delivery (FTD)

CoverGirl Cosmetics

Apple

United Airlines

C Ask and answer the questions with a partner.

1. What kinds of companies are listed in **B**?

2. What do they produce, or what service do they offer?

3. Which slogan do you like best? Why? Which slogan promotes its company the best?

4. Which slogan is your least favorite? Why?

5. Imagine you can invest some money in one of these companies. Which one would you choose? Which one(s) would you avoid? Why?

7 WELLBEING

Look at the photo. Answer the questions.

1 What is the person in the photo doing?

2 In your opinion, is this activity good for your health? Do you ever do it?

3 What are some things you do to stay healthy?

UNIT GOALS

1 Describe symptoms when you don't feel well

2 Give, accept, and reject serious health advice

3 Talk about modern health problems

4 Describe health tips you've been given

A jogger goes for a run on a cool autumn day in Berlin, Germany.

Two friends fist-bump

1 VIDEO Is it Better to Shake (Hands) or (Fist) Bump?

A 🔎 Look up these words in your dictionary: *bacteria*, *germs*, *transmit*, *disease*. Then read the title of the video. What do you think this video is going to be about? Tell a partner.

B ▶ Watch the beginning of the video. Complete the questions. How would you answer them?

Is handshaking the _____ or _____ way of saying hello? Could there be another _____?
What about the _____ _____?

C ▶ Watch the entire video. You are going to hear about a doctor named Tom McClellan. He did a study about handshaking and fist-bumping. Listen and complete the outline.

1. The situation
   A. In the _____, we shake hands all day.
   B. You can _____ diseases when you shake hands.
2. The study
   A. We shook hands with _____ different workers.
   B. We checked to see how many _____ we'd collected.
   C. We repeated the process with fist-bumping.
3. The results
   A. There was _____ times the amount of bacteria on hand shakers.

D 🔎 What do you think of Dr. McClellan's study? After watching the video, are you going to change your behavior in any way? Tell a partner.

2 VOCABULARY

A Read part of a story below. What do the words in **blue** mean?

Adventure on a Mountain by Michael Yamato

There were more than 20 climbers on the mountain that day. We had been climbing for hours. My partner, Ed, and I were trying to reach the top before noon.

It was freezing, and the winds were strong. We were both wet and cold. Worst of all, a big storm was approaching.

That's when the trouble began. Ed started to get **drowsy**. He kept saying, "I just want to sleep." He was talking, but I couldn't understand him clearly—he wasn't **making sense**. The air was very thin, and I felt **dizzy**, too, but Ed was *really* confused. His steps were heavy. He was obviously **exhausted**.

Ed's body was very cold. Then he started to **shiver** uncontrollably. His **breathing** was slowing down. I was getting scared. I **felt weak**, too, but suddenly my own weakness disappeared. I had a lot of energy and knew that I needed to help Ed. It was then that I remembered the dry clothes and warm drinks in my backpack...

Match the words with their meanings.

1. drowsy _e_

2. make sense ____

3. dizzy ____

4. exhausted ____

5. shiver ____

6. breathe ____

7. weak ____

a. not strong	d. very tired
b. to shake because of the cold	e. ~~sleepy~~
c. to be clear or understandable	f. to take air into your body
	g. unable to balance

B 🔁 Now answer the questions about the story in **A** on a separate piece of paper. Compare your answers with a partner's.

1. Where were Michael and Ed? How did they feel at first?

2. What happened to Ed next?

3. What do you think they should have done? (Give a reason to support your answer.)

   ☐ continued to the top   ☐ waited for help   ☐ turned back

4. How do you think the story ended?

C Here are some more words about health. (You might hear these sentences in a doctor's office.) Can you match each word in **blue** with one or more parts of the body on the right?

1. Don't **chew** the medicine—just **swallow** it with some water. _____, _____

2. Look straight ahead. Try not to **blink**. _____

3. Please relax and just **breathe** normally. _____

4. Please cover your mouth when you **cough**. _____

chest

eyes

mouth

nose

teeth

throat

3 LISTENING

A  **Make predictions.** Which word do you think makes the statement true? Discuss with a partner.

1. _____ too much is bad for your health.

    a. Sitting   b. Standing   c. Running

B 🔊 **Check predictions.** Listen to the conversation. What did Lea learn? Circle the correct answer in **A**. CD 2 Track 2

C 🔊 **Listen for details.** Listen again. Choose the correct answer for each question. For some items, more than one answer is correct. CD 2 Track 2

1. How did Lea describe her symptoms?

    a. Her back was hurting.   b. She felt dizzy.   c. She had neck pain.

2. What did the doctor do?

    a. He sent her to the hospital.   b. He asked her a question.   c. He did some tests.

3. How many total hours a day was Lea sitting?

    a. 9–10   b. 11–12   c. 14–15

4. How can sitting be bad for your health?

    a. It can make it hard to go to sleep.   c. It can make your muscles hurt.

    b. It can affect your energy.   d. It can give you headaches.

D 🔊 **Infer information.** Listen to these lines from the audio. Choose the correct answer for each item. CD 2 Track 3

1. Why did Lea say "no kidding" to Cooper?

    a. She was saying, "I'm surprised."

    b. She was saying, "I agree with you."

2. Why did the doctor ask Lea the strange question?

    a. He couldn't find anything else wrong with her.

    b. He didn't believe her symptoms.

3. Why did Lea say "you got it" to Cooper?

    a. To tell Cooper that he understood correctly.

    b. To tell Cooper that he might be sick, too.

Studies show that people who spend time each day outside feel healthier and more energized.

E  It's important to be active. What are one or two simple things you can do to sit less and be more active during the day? Share your answers with a partner.

4 SPEAKING

A 🔊 Ming wants to join the school swim team. Before she can do that, she has to get a checkup from her doctor. Listen to and read the conversation. Then answer the questions below. **CD 2 Track 4**

1. What expressions does the doctor use to give advice? Underline them.

2. Do you think the language is formal or informal?

DR. PENA: OK, Ming, we're finished. As far as I can tell, you're completely healthy!

MING: Great!

DR. PENA: But I do want to talk to you about one thing.

MING: Uh-oh. This doesn't sound good.

DR. PENA: No, it's nothing scary. It's just that winter is coming. You need to prepare. I always advise my patients to get a flu shot.

MING: Hmm... I could never do that. I'm afraid of needles!

DR. PENA: Don't worry, Ming. The shot doesn't hurt at all.

MING: Really? Well, maybe...

DR. PENA: It will protect you from the flu. You'll be able to swim all year without getting sick. In my opinion, I think you should do it.

MING: Well, OK. Maybe I'll give it a try.

DR. PENA: Good! I'll tell the nurse to come in and see you. Take care and good luck on the swim team this year!

B 🔁 Practice the conversation with a partner.

SPEAKING STRATEGY

C 🔁 Look at the two photos to the right. Work with a partner and answer these questions.

1. What's happened in each photo?

2. How does each person feel?

 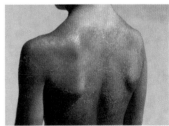

D 🔁 Choose one of the situations in **C** and write a conversation. Work with your partner. Use the Useful Expressions to help you.

Student A: You are a helpful person.

Student B: You have the problem.

A: Excuse me. Are you all right?

B: I'm not sure.

A: What happened?

B: I fell off my bike.

A: Are you dizzy? I think you should call a doctor.

Useful Expressions	
Giving serious advice	
In my opinion, you should...	I think the best idea (for you) is to...
I always advise people to...	If I were you, I'd...
Accepting advice	**Refusing advice**
You're right. Thanks for the advice.	I'm not sure that would work for me.
That makes (a lot of) sense. I'll give it a try.	That doesn't (really) make sense to me.
I'll try it and get back to you.	I could never do that.

E 👥 Perform your conversation for the class.

5 GRAMMAR

A Turn to page 206. Complete the exercises. Then do **B–E** below.

Describing Symptoms					
have	**Noun**		**Possessive adjective**	**Noun**	***hurt***
I	have	a headache,	and	my	throat	hurts.
feel / be	**Adjective**			***can't stop***	***-ing* verb**
I	feel / am	tired,	and	I	can't stop	shivering.

Other common vocabulary

have + noun: I have (a stomachache / an earache / a backache / a toothache / a cut / a sore throat / a fever / a temperature / a cold / the flu).

possessive adjective + noun + hurt: My (arm / finger / back / stomach) hurts. My (legs) hurt.

feel / be + adjective: I feel / am (dizzy / nauseous / drowsy / exhausted / faint / weak / sick).

can't stop + -ing verb: I can't stop (coughing / scratching / sneezing).

B 🔊 **Pronunciation: The schwa sound.** Listen and repeat. Underline the vowels that use a schwa sound. **CD 2 Track 5**

1. I have a cold.
2. I was coughing all the time.
3. I think I have the flu.
4. And my stomach hurts.

C Think of a time when you or someone you know was sick. On a piece of paper, write four sentences about the symptoms.

> I didn't feel well.
>
> I couldn't stop coughing.
>
> My chest was hurting.
>
> I couldn't swallow food.

D 🔄 Role-play with a partner. One student is the patient, and the other student is the doctor.

Patient: Imagine you are sick now. Describe your symptoms to the doctor.

Doctor: Listen to the symptoms. Give the patient some advice.

> Doctor, I don't feel well at all. I think I may have a fever, too.

> Well, let's see. You do have a temperature. What other symptoms do you have?

> My chest hurts, and I can't stop coughing. It's impossible for me to sleep at night.

E 🔄 Switch roles and do the role play again.

6 COMMUNICATION

A What do you know about the treatments below? Would you ever try them? Tell a partner.

B In groups of four, role-play the following situations.

Student A: Think of a health problem. Tell your partners at least three of your symptoms.

Students B–D: Give Student A advice about the problem. Each student should recommend a different treatment: massage, yoga, meditation, or some other treatment. You can use the notes and example below to help you.

Massage	Meditation
+ used to treat aches and pains	+ helps with relaxation
+ increases your flexibility	+ has been done for thousands of years
+ can help with your mood	+ can be done alone or in a group
– can be expensive	– can be frustrating or boring
Yoga	**A treatment of your choice:**
+ a good way to exercise	+
+ emphasizes breath control	+
+ no special equipment necessary	+
– can be physically challenging	–

A: I'm having trouble sleeping.

B: In my opinion, you should try meditation.

A: Really? Have you tried it?

B: Absolutely. It really helps with relaxation.

A: I'm not sure that would work for me. It sounds kind of boring.

C: If I were you, I'd try yoga because…

C Student A chooses the treatment he or she prefers and explains why. Then switch roles and perform the role play again. Repeat until everyone has had a chance to play Student A.

1 VOCABULARY

A  Work with a partner. Look at the Word Bank. Then do the following.

1. Each person should take one person's comment below and read it aloud with feeling.

2. Then explain the person's situation in your own words. Your partner will give you some advice.

Word Bank
Word partnerships with *sick*
be / feel sick = be / feel ill
be sick of (something) = be tired of (something)
be worried sick = be very worried
call in sick = call your work to say you are ill
sick days = days you can take off from work when you are ill

CAROLINA: My favorite band is playing on Saturday night, but I have class until 6:00, and then I have to work. I'm thinking about **cutting class** and **calling in sick** to work so I can go to the concert. I'm doing well in my class, and I have a lot of **sick days** left, so I don't have to worry.

JILL: I'm **sick of** my parents **bossing** me **around**. I'm supposed to be at home right after school, but yesterday I came home late. My mother said she was **worried sick** about me. Now she's **grounded** me—I can't go out with my friends for a week. My parents **treat** me like a baby even though I'm 16 years old! I can **take care** of myself!

B Read the pieces of advice below. Who does each one apply to: Carolina or Jill? Write the name.

1. Try to follow the rules. Your parents worry because they **care about** you. _____

2. You have a **well paid** job. You don't want to lose it. I think you should go to work. _____

3. You **might as well** listen to your parents. If you don't, they'll just get upset. _____

4. If you're a good student, talk to your instructor. He might understand. _____

C  Ask and answer the questions with a partner.

1. Have you (or someone you know) ever cut class? called in sick to work? been worried sick about something? been grounded? Why?

2. What's something you're sick of?

3. Do your parents or older siblings ever boss you around or treat you like a baby?

2 LISTENING

A 🔊 **Infer information.** Read the question below. Then listen and answer it. **CD 2 Track 6**

Which two things are probably true about Ben? Circle them.

a. He lives at home with his parents.

b. He studies at a school in another city.

c. He is getting ready to graduate from college.

d. He just started college recently.

B 🔊 **Listen for feeling.** Listen. How does Ben feel about the three topics below? Write the correct letter next to each topic. (One item is extra.) **CD 2 Track 6**

1. math class _____
2. roommate _____
3. the soccer team _____

a. He likes it / him.

b. He doesn't like it / him.

c. He's not sure about it / him.

d. He used to like it / him.

C 🔊 **Listen for details.** Listen again. Which words describe Ben? someone else? If you checked *someone else*, who is being described in each case? **CD 2 Track 6**

	Ben	Someone else	Person described
1. an early riser	☐	☑	Ben's mother
2. homesick	☐	☐	
3. well behaved	☐	☐	
4. not feeling well	☐	☐	
5. at home after 8:00	☐	☐	

D 🔄 Think about a time you were in a new situation. Describe how you felt to a partner.

3 READING

A  Can modern life make you sick? If yes, how? Tell a partner.

B 🔄 **Scan for information; Make predictions.** Copy the chart below on a piece of paper. Then scan the article. What are the names of the five medical conditions mentioned? Write the answers in the chart under *Syndrome*. When you have this problem, what do you think happens? Tell a partner.

Syndrome	Description	Possible solution
1. CHAOS	You feel embarrassed because your house is messy.	
2.		
3.		
4.		
5.		

C **Check predictions; Read for details.** Now read the article. Complete the chart above with the description and possible solution for each syndrome. If a solution is not mentioned, write *NM*.

D 🔄 **Infer meaning.** What do the words below mean? Find them in the passage. Then work with a partner to guess the definitions. Check a dictionary for the answers.

1st paragraph: *tidy* _____

2nd paragraph: *fatigue* _____

3rd paragraph: *rushing* _____

5th paragraph: *gentle* _____

E 🔄 Look at where you wrote *NM* in the chart in **B**. Can you suggest some possible solutions?

Which syndrome is the worst? Why? Take a vote as a class.

MODERN HEALTH PROBLEMS

Margaret's friend is taking a new job in a faraway city. Margaret wants to have a goodbye dinner party at her home. But she can't. Margaret suffers from **CHAOS** *(Can't Have Anyone Over Syndrome)*. Her apartment is messy, and she's embarrassed by it. "I've never been a tidy person," she says. "My best friend gave me some good advice. He told me to get a house cleaner."

These days we get and receive so much information every day. People call, text, and email us all day long, and they expect quick responses from us. It can be very demanding—and it's making some people sick. They have **information fatigue syndrome**. There is so much information, they become paralyzed[1] and can't think clearly. "I can't

[1]If you are *paralyzed*, you cannot move.

sleep at night because I worry," says Bahman, a college senior. "I'm sick of it."

Do you sometimes engage in *deskfast* (eating breakfast at your desk at work)? If your answer is *yes*, then you may suffer from hurry sickness. **Hurry sickness** is a straightforward name for another syndrome of modern life. "I'm always rushing. And I'm tired all the time. Just last week I had to call in sick because I was so stressed," says Mari, a company employee. "I'm worried about using all of my sick days."

We've all complained about having too much work to do. Well, how about not having enough work? **Underload syndrome** is caused by having little or nothing to do at the office. Steven works

as a project manager. "I can finish my work in about four hours, but I'm afraid to say anything about it. I don't want to be assigned too much work!" So what does he do? Steven pretends to be busy. "I'm thinking about getting a part-time job in the evening. That's one possible idea."

Chances are you've experienced **text neck** before. Another name for it would be *pain in the neck*, because that's what people with this condition experience. Looking down at your phone and texting for a long time causes *text neck*. How can you take care of it? Getting a gentle neck massage—nothing too hard—will help you relax and feel better.

4 GRAMMAR

A Turn to page 207. Complete the exercises. Then do **B–D** below.

Reported Speech: Commands and Requests		
	Quoted speech	**Reported speech**
Command	The doctor said, "Get some rest." The doctor said, "Don't smoke."	The doctor **told** <u>me</u> **to get** some rest. The doctor **told** <u>him</u> **not to smoke**.
Request	Jon said, "Please turn off <u>your</u> phone." Maria asked, "Can <u>you</u> help <u>me</u>?"	Jon **asked** <u>me</u> **to turn off** <u>my</u> phone. Maria **asked** <u>us</u> **to help** <u>her</u>.

B Take three small pieces of paper. Do the following.

- On one piece of paper, write a command in quoted speech.

- On a second piece of paper, write a second command in quoted speech. It should use *not*.

- On a third piece of paper, write a request in quoted speech.

> My mom said, "Come home after school."

> The teacher said to the students, "Don't cut class."

> Jin asked, "Can you open the door?"

C 👥 Work in a small group. Follow the steps below.

1. Put all your papers together and mix them. Put them face down on the desk in a pile.

2. One person begins. Turn over a paper. You have 15 seconds to make a reported speech statement using the sentence on the paper.

> My mom told me to come home after school.

3. If you make a correct reported statement, you get a point. Then put the paper aside. If you can't make a correct statement, put the paper at the bottom of the pile.

4. Then the next person goes. Play until you use all the papers. Who has the most points?

D 👥 Take your three sentences and get together with a new group. Repeat **C**.

5 WRITING

When I was in high school, my dad always told me to exercise and eat healthy food. He did these things, but I didn't. I was too busy with my studies, and I didn't have time to exercise. I ate a lot of junk food and didn't treat my body well, so I gained weight. Six months ago, I started college, and I decided to make a change. First, I joined a gym. Then I asked a trainer to help me with a diet and exercise plan. I started eating better and exercising more. Today, I'm doing well. I'm five kilos lighter, and I have more energy. Too bad I didn't listen to my dad's advice in high school. He was right!

A 🔄 Read the paragraph on page 106. Answer the questions with a partner.

1. What health advice did the writer get and from whom?

2. Did the writer follow that advice? Why or why not?

3. Does the writer think it was good advice? Why or why not?

B Think of health advice you've gotten for living a happy and healthy life. It could be from a person (like a parent or doctor) or from another source (like a magazine). Answer questions 1–3 in **A**. Then use your notes and the example to help you write a paragraph of your own.

C 🔄 Exchange your writing with a partner. Read his or her paragraph.

1. Are there any mistakes? If yes, circle them.

2. Answer questions 1–3 in **A** about your partner's writing.

3. Return the paper to your partner. Make corrections to your own paragraph.

6 COMMUNICATION

A Look at the tips for leading a healthy and happy life. Add four more tips to the list.

Tips for leading a healthy and happy life			
Get plenty of rest.	Eat healthy foods.		
Spend time with good friends.	Don't hang out with negative people.		

B 👥 Ask three different classmates: "What is important for a healthy and happy life?" Write their names and answers in the chart.

Name	Answer
1.	
2.	
3.	

C 👥 Get into small groups. Take turns reporting what your classmates said. Do you agree with their advice? Why or why not?

> Pablo told me to eat a big breakfast every morning.

> Yuki told me not to worry about my exams too much.

D 👥 Review all the advice you got in **B**. Together, choose the three best tips and share your answers with the class.

8 THE ACTIVE LIFE

Look at the photo. Answer the questions.

1 What is this person doing? Have you ever done this activity?

2 What do you do to stay active?

3 What is one popular leisure time activity in your country?

UNIT GOALS

1 Talk about things you do to stay active

2 Explain the set-up and rules of a game

3 Talk about how long you've done certain activities

4 Describe a favorite activity in detail

A man in-line skates at the Oscar Niemeyer International Cultural Center in Aviles, Spain.

LESSON **A** **LEISURE TIME**

A rock climber on a cliff in Oman

1 VIDEO Rock Climbing in Oman

A ▶ You are going to watch a video about some rock climbers. Watch with the sound off and complete the climbers' names. Then answer the question: Do you know where Oman is?

_____ Synnott, expedition leader and climber   _____ Honnold, climber

_____ Chin, photographer   _____ Findlay, climber

B ▶ Now watch again with the sound on. Choose the correct answer for each item.

1. *Soloing* means *climbing without a* _____.

   a. rope   b. partner

2. It can be dangerous because _____.

   a. the water can hurt when you land in it

   b. the rocks can hurt when they land on you in the water

3. The climbers are telling stories about people who have _____.

   a. succeeded   b. died

4. Alex and Hazel are pushing Mark because they are _____ climbers.

   a. veteran   b. younger

5. Mark says, "I'm doing this for the _____."

   a. money   b. adventure

C 🔄 Which of these things would you try? Tell a partner.

   a. rock climbing   b. diving from a high place   c. visiting Oman

WORLD LINK

Go online and find one interesting fact about Oman to share with the class.

2 VOCABULARY

A Read about the person below. Do you know anybody like this?

Some parents worry that their children spend too much time playing games online.

Word Bank

activity

be involved in an / participate in an / take part in an ~

spare / leisure time ~

physical, mental, outdoor, extracurricular, classroom ~

active

stay / remain ~

highly / extremely / very ~

fairly, increasingly ~

mentally, physically ~

athlete

amateur, professional, serious ~

This is my friend. He's really **into** playing video games online. In his spare time, he plays games ten hours a day, seven days a week. He **takes part in** competitions every couple of months and has even won money playing!

He started out playing only on weekends, but became more **active** as his skill level increased. He even watches videos of other players to remain as up-to-date as possible. He knows a lot of other gamers, and they share tips online.

The game requires a lot of mental activity, but his mother worries he isn't **physically active**. She would also like to see him **participate in** some **extracurricular activities** at school, not just be on his computer all the time. He argues that he is **fairly active**, and the game gives him a chance to **be involved in** a team.

B Circle T for *True* or F for *False*. Explain your answers to a partner.

1. I take part in an online community.	T	F
2. I think it's OK to spend a lot of time online.	T	F
3. It's strange to make money from playing video games.	T	F
4. Video games can keep you mentally active.	T	F
5. It's important to spend some time outdoors every day.	T	F

C Answer the questions with your partner.

1. What do you do to stay active?

2. What things do you like to do in your spare time?

3 LISTENING

A 🔊 **Pronunciation: Stress in compound nouns.** A compound noun is a phrase or word made up of more than one noun. Listen and repeat. **CD 2 Track 8**

1. BOARD game   2. BASKETball   3. COMPUTER game

B 🔊 🔄 **Pronunciation: Stress in compound nouns.** Look at the underlined compound nouns. Circle the stressed word in each one. Then listen and practice saying the sentences with a partner. **CD 2 Track 9**

1. Sergei is the national <u>table tennis</u> champion.

2. I want to stay active, so I got a <u>gym membership</u>.

3. How many <u>comic books</u> does he have?

4. I need to practice to get my <u>driver's license</u> in my spare time.

5. I've put the best photos in my <u>photo album</u>.

6. She's good at <u>baseball</u>.

C Read the two definitions for *renew*. Then match each definition (1 or 2) with a sentence (a or b).

> 1. You can **renew** (= begin again) an activity or relationship.
>
> 2. You can also **renew** (= extend the time period of) documents.

    a. Members can renew their museum membership online.

    b. I saw him for the first time in 20 years, and we renewed our friendship.

D 🔊 **Listen for details; Infer information.** You will hear a couple of conversations between two people. Read the items below. Then listen and select the best response to each question. **CD 2 Track 10**

Conversation 1

1. What is Andy calling Lucia about?
   a. her gym membership
   b. a new gym
   c. a workout plan

2. How much is Andy offering?
   a. 40 percent off
   b. 20 percent off
   c. 20 dollars off

3. What can be inferred?
   a. Lucia exercises too much.
   b. Lucia paid already.
   c. Lucia hasn't met Andy before.

Conversation 2

1. What does Deo want to do?
   a. drive more on the weekends
   b. get rid of his car
   c. take his car to work

2. What can be inferred?
   a. It's easy to shop in Deo's neighborhood.
   b. Deo's car is popular.
   c. Deo doesn't pay for parking.

3. What will Deo probably not do?
   a. sell his car
   b. renew his license
   c. get a new car

E 🔄 Check your answers in **D** with a partner. Then think about one of the decisions from the conversations. What do you think of the decision? Tell your partner.

4 SPEAKING

A 🔊 🔁 Rohan is telling Ana about cricket, a game that he likes to play. Listen to and practice the conversation with a partner. Then complete the sentences below. **CD 2 Track 11**

ROHAN: Cricket is a great game. I love it!

ANA: I've never heard of it.

ROHAN: Oh, it's really popular, especially in England, India, and some other countries in Asia.

ANA: Well, how do you play?

ROHAN: It's played with a bat and a ball. Oh, and you need gloves, too. You start by pitching the ball to the striker.[1]

ANA: It sounds like baseball to me.

ROHAN: They're similar. But in cricket, there are 11 players on a team. And you play on an oval field.

ANA: How do you win?

ROHAN: The object of the game is to get more runs than the other team, and... Hey, what time is it?

ANA: Four o'clock. Why?

ROHAN: I have to go. I'm late for cricket practice!

[1]*the striker* = the hitter

1. Cricket is similar to _____.

2. Each team has _____ players.

3. The team with the most _____ wins.

4. You need a _____, a _____, and _____ to play.

SPEAKING STRATEGY

B 👥 Look at the photo and read about the game of bocce. With a partner, write a conversation similar to the one in **A**. Use the Useful Expressions to help you. Perform your conversation for another pair.

<u>What you need:</u>

- a small ball
- several bigger balls
- two teams of 1–4 people each

<u>How to play:</u>

- First, throw the small ball down the field.
- Each team then rolls the bigger balls down the field.
- Score a point for the big ball that is closest to the small ball.
- The team with the most points wins!

Useful Expressions: Explaining the set-up and rules of a game	
Equipment	It's played with... / You don't need any special equipment.
People	There are 11 players on each team. / You compete against each other.
Playing the game	One team starts by... / The game begins when...
How to win	The team with the most points wins. / The object is to score the most runs.
Location	It's played on a field. / It's played all over the world.

5 GRAMMAR

A Turn to page 208. Complete the exercises. Then do **B** and **C** below.

The Present Perfect vs. the Present Perfect Continuous
I**'ve played** cricket <u>since I was a child</u>. = I**'ve been playing** cricket <u>since I was a child</u>.
I**'ve read** a book about long-distance running. It was excellent. (The action is completed.) ≠ I**'ve been reading** a book about long-distance running. I'm enjoying it. (The action is ongoing.)

I**'ve been going** to the gym a lot <u>lately</u>.	<u>Recently</u> I**'ve been working out** more.
~~I've been owning that car for ten years.~~	I**'ve owned** that car for ten years.
~~I've been taking this test three times already.~~	I**'ve taken** this test three times already.

B On a piece of paper, answer the questions using the present perfect or present perfect continuous tense.

1. What is one extracurricular activity you've participated in this year?
2. What is one you've been participating in recently?

3. Name someone who has moved recently.
4. Name someone who has been living in the same place for a long time.

5. What celebrity has received a lot of attention from the media?
6. What celebrity have people been talking about lately?

7. What is one helpful thing you've learned in school?
8. What is something you've been studying for a long time, but don't really like?

9. What is one classroom activity you've disliked?
10. What is one you've been enjoying recently?

C Now ask a partner the questions in **B**. Ask follow-up questions to get more information.

What is one extracurricular activity you've participated in this year?

I've been a member of the drama club. It's a lot of fun.

What do you like about it?

6 COMMUNICATION

A Write about two things you started doing in the past and still do today.

> I've been making model airplanes since I was a little kid.

> I've been learning how to cook French food for the past year.

1. _____

2. _____

B Get into a group of three people. Follow the steps below.

1. Look at the sentences each student wrote in **A**. Choose one sentence to talk about.

2. Ask the student who wrote the sentence as many questions as possible about the sentence. You will have two minutes to learn everything you can.

C Take turns playing a guessing game as a class. Follow the steps below.

1. Now the group of three students stands in front of the class. All three students say the sentence they chose in **B**. Two students lie, but they want the class to believe that they are the ones who have had the experience.

> I've been learning how to cook French food for the past year.

2. The other students in the class ask the members of the group questions. They have two minutes to find out which student is telling the truth, and which two are lying.

> Dmitri, what's your favorite French food?

> Carmen, what's one dish you've learned to make?

> Kumiko, who has taught you how to cook French food?

Jorge Jones is spending the next year taking his motorcycle down the PanAmerican Highway and visiting all the countries and cultures along the way.

1 VOCABULARY

A 🔁 Look at the words in **blue** in the interview below. Which do you know already? Tell a partner.

B 🔁 Look at the photo and read the caption. Then read the interview aloud with your partner. One person is the interviewer. The other person is Jorge Jones. Then answer the questions in your own words.

1. What is Jorge doing?
2. How did he prepare for it?
3. Why is he doing it?

How did you prepare for this trip?

Before I **headed out**, I went on several long hikes. I also saved all my money to **pay for** the trip, and now I'm very careful about what I **spend** my money **on**. Since I started the trip, I've also talked with local guides in different places, too. They know about a given area and can share stories and tips about it.

Isn't it dangerous?

I've been **warned about** some places. I've had some trouble, but I'm not afraid to **ask for** help or change plans if necessary.

What are you looking forward to?

I'm looking forward to **staying in** all these places and **learning about** different Latin American cultures. I want to spend time with people whose stories are not well known and share those stories with the world.

Why are you doing this now?

This is a great opportunity for me to learn about myself and the world. I **believe in** the idea that we have more in common than differences between us. I am excited to learn about indigenous* cultures and see all of the natural beauty of Latin America.

---

*indigenous = native to a region

C 🔁 Imagine you are traveling around the world. Take turns asking and answering the questions with a partner.

1. How would you prepare for the trip? Who would you ask for help?
2. Who would you like to travel with? Which cities would you stay in?
3. During your travels, what would you spend the most money on?

2 LISTENING

A 🔄 Is there an activity that you've always wanted to try? What is it? Tell a partner.

B 🔊 **Listen for gist.** Listen to the beginning of the conversation. What activities are part of parkour?
CD 2 Track 12

running   mountain biking   swimming   jumping   climbing

C 🔊 **Listen for details.** Listen to the conversation. Circle the correct sentence (a or b).
CD 2 Track 13

1. a. The man will run, jump, and climb in cities and parks.

   b. The man will run, jump, and climb in stadiums.

2. a. The man is careful and studies an area before he starts.

   b. The man starts and deals with challenges when he sees them.

3. a. There is a paramedic nearby if something bad happens.

   b. His friend has a first-aid kit and phone if something bad happens.

4. a. The purpose of the trip is to accomplish a goal and show people a way to be active.

   b. The purpose of the trip is to get from one place to another.

D 🔄 Would you like to try this activity? Why or why not? Tell a partner.

3 READING

A 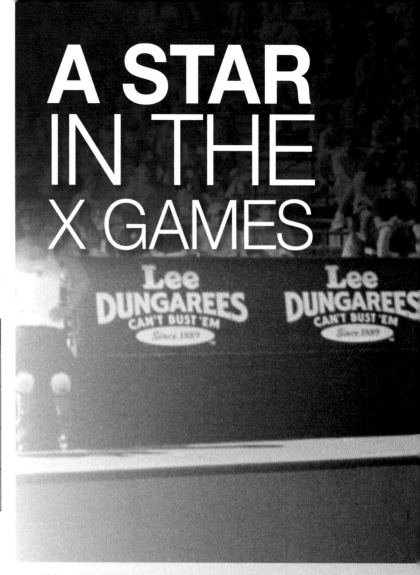 **Use background knowledge.** Look at the title of the article and the photo. Ask and answer these questions with a partner.

1. Have you ever heard of the X Games?
2. Can you name any sports that are played at these games?

B **Scan for information.** Look quickly at the article. Add at least two examples to each item in the chart below.

Item	Examples
1. summer sports	
2. winter sports	
3. regional teams in the global championships	
4. categories of in-line skating	

C **Read for details.** Read the statements about Fabiola. Then find a sentence in the reading that supports each statement.

1. Fabiola's mom didn't make a lot of money. _____

2. Fabiola wins against women.

   _____

3. Fabiola wins against men.

   _____

4. Fabiola is well known outside her own country. _____

5. Fabiola has her own sense of style.

   _____

D Who are some popular female athletes you know? What sports do they play? Which would you rather see, the Olympics or the X Games? Why? Discuss with a partner.

A STAR IN THE X GAMES

When the X Games first started out, they were not well known. Only a few people watched and competed in them. However, the Games had an attitude and style that reflected things many young people cared about, and in time, they became popular around the world.

In different areas of the world, athletes train and compete in their own versions of the X Games. The best athletes can advance to the global championship. At the championship, teams from six regions (Asia, Australia, Canada, Europe, South America, and the United States) face each other. There are summer sports (in-line skating, biking, and skateboarding) and winter ones (skiing and snowboarding). The sports are so popular that some are even in the Olympics now!

There are many champions in the X Games, but one woman, Fabiola da Silva, has always stood

out from the crowd. She's an in-line skater from Brazil, and she's easily recognizable with her tank top and nose ring.

There are two different in-line skating categories: *park* and *vert*. In the park event, skaters compete on a course that has ledges, handrails, and other obstacles. In the vert event, skaters do tricks on a half-pipe[1]. They try to fly high in the air and spin. Fabiola competes in both events and has won six gold medals in the vert event, her specialty. She has been skating for years and has dominated[2] the women's events.

Fabiola is a pioneer. She was one of the first women to get very famous from the X Games, but she's not afraid of the guys. Ever since she received her first pair of skates at the age of 12, she's played with boys. Now she skates in competitions with them, and she beats many of them.

Fabiola's mother was a housekeeper and life was hard, but she saved her money to buy Fabiola's skates. It was a good investment. Fabiola has traveled abroad for events and has become famous in the international skating world.

Success hasn't gone to her head[3], though. She's still a typical young woman: she has a boyfriend, likes to listen to rock music, and prefers healthy foods. And she doesn't seem to care much about the attention she gets.

[1]A *half-pipe* is a curved structure with high sides, used for doing tricks.
[2]If you *dominate*, you are powerful and successful.
[3]If something *goes to your head*, it makes you think you are very important.

4 GRAMMAR

A Turn to page 209. Complete the exercises. Then do **B–D** below.

Review: The Simple Past vs. the Present Perfect vs. the Present Perfect Continuous		
	Completed past action	Actions started in the past continuing up to now
Simple past	I **visited** South Africa <u>in 2010</u>.	
Present perfect	**I've visited** South Africa once.	Fabiola **has skated** for years.
Present perfect continuous		Fabiola **has been skating** for years.

B With a partner, complete the chart with the names of famous people you know something about.

Actors	
Singers	
Athletes	
Others (your idea)	

C With the same partner, choose one of the famous people in **B**. Complete the sentences about him or her. Then write the questions you would ask to get that information.

Sentences	Questions
1. I was born in _____.	When / Where were you born?
2. I became famous because _____.	
3. I've _____ since _____. I've been _____ for _____.	
4. I got interested in _____ when I _____.	
5. I've recently been in the news because _____.	

D Join another pair. Use the questions in **C** to interview the other pair. You might need to change some questions. Can you guess their famous person's name?

> How long have you been playing baseball professionally?

> I've been playing for five years.

5 WRITING

A 🔄 Read the paragraphs. Answer the questions with a partner.

1. What is the writer's hobby?

2. How long has she been doing it?

3. Was she good at the activity at first? Is she good at it now?

4. Why does she like the activity?

> My hobby is rock climbing. I've been doing it for a year. In the beginning, I wasn't very good, but I've gotten better.
>
> I started rock climbing in high school. I went to an indoor place with my friends. On the first day, I was really nervous, so I only climbed low rocks. It was hard, but fun. I kept working, and now I can climb very fast. I even climb outside now.
>
> I like rock climbing because it helps me stay in shape. It's also a good way to make friends. I've met a lot of people. We climb, but we also hang out and spend time doing other things now.

B What is your hobby? Answer the questions in **A**. Then use your notes and the example to help you write three paragraphs of your own.

C 🔄 Exchange your writing with a partner. Read his or her paragraphs.

1. Are there any mistakes? If yes, circle them.

2. Answer the questions in **A** about your partner's writing.

3. Return the paper to your partner. Make corrections to your own paragraphs.

6 COMMUNICATION

A Write the four questions from Writing **A** so they are in the second person (*you*) form.

1. What is your hobby? _____

2. _____

3. _____

4. _____

B 👥 Interview six classmates using the questions in **A**. Take notes on their answers.

C 🔄 Work with a partner. Answer the questions.

In your class…

> How long have you been doing it?

> Since last year.

1. which hobbies are the most popular?

2. which hobby is the most interesting or unusual?

3. who's been doing his or her hobby the longest?

9 SOCIAL ISSUES

Look at the photo. Answer the questions.

1 What problems do you see in the photo?

2 Do these things happen where you live?

3 What is an important social issue (problem) where you live?

UNIT GOALS

1 Give a short formal presentation

2 State the purpose and important points of your presentation

3 Discuss environmental and social problems

4 Make predictions and talk about consequences

Traffic in downtown Bangkok, Thailand

Apartment buildings in Hong Kong, one of the *megacities* of the world.

1 VIDEO Seven Billion

A Currently, over 7 billion people live on Earth, and the number is increasing. Do you think this is a problem? Why or why not? Discuss with a partner.

B ▶ Work with a partner. Read the questions and guess the answers. Then watch the video to check your guesses.

1. It would take 2 / 20 / 200 years just to count to 7 billion out loud.

2. In 2045, the world's population could be 9 / 12 / 15 billion.

3. In 2010, the average person lived 53 / 61 / 69 years.

4. In 1960, the average person lived 53 / 61 / 69 years.

5. In 1975, the world's three megacities were New York City, Tokyo, and Mexico City / Rome / Sydney.

6. Right now there are 7 / 14 / 21 megacities in the world.

7. By 2050, 50 / 70 / 90% of us will be living in cities.

8. Seven billion people, speaking 7,000 languages, living in 19 / 94 / 194 countries.

C Read these statistics from the end of the video. Which one is the biggest problem and why? Discuss with a partner.

5% of the population consumes 23% of the world's energy.

13% of the people in the world don't have clean drinking water.

38% of the world's population lacks adequate sanitation.

WORLD LINK

Go online and find one other problem that population growth is causing in the world. Report back to the class.

2 VOCABULARY

A 🔄 Doris Chavez and Amelia Smith are running for mayor. Read their ads. Then answer the questions by checking the correct box(es) with a partner.

DORIS CHAVEZ for mayor!

"We're making progress in many areas. Why change now? Reelect Doris Chavez!"

In her first term, Mayor Chavez:
- launched a new school lunch program for elementary school students.
- taxed large companies to raise extra money.
- worked enthusiastically to improve life for everyone—crime is down 30%.

There is no better candidate than Doris Chavez for mayor!

AMELIA SMITH for mayor! ★ ★ ★ ★ ★ ★

"No more politics as usual. It's time for change in our city! Vote for Amelia Smith!"

Amelia Smith vows:
- to expand the school lunch program to include older students.
- not to raise taxes on corporations.
- to work hard for all citizens to keep our city streets safe.

★★★★★★★★★★★★★★★★★★★★★★★★★

Amelia Smith is the clear choice for mayor!

	Doris	Amelia
1. Who is currently the mayor?	☐	☐
2. Who doesn't want to increase taxes?	☐	☐
3. Who is interested in the school lunch program?	☐	☐
4. Who mentions crime and safety?	☐	☐

B Look at the information in **A**. Write the word(s) in blue next to their definitions.

1. doing (something) the same way: _____as usual_____

2. eagerly, with great energy: _____

3. a fixed period of time: _____

4. increase in size: _____

5. large companies: _____

6. started: _____

7. promises: _____

8. moving forward: _____

9. obvious: _____

10. a person who is competing for a position: _____

11. members of a city or country: _____

12. made someone pay money to the government: _____

C 🔄 Discuss the questions with a partner.

1. Do you ever see ads like the ones in **A**? How else do politicians campaign where you live?

2. Think of a person who was up for reelection recently. Did people vote for or against him or her? Why?

3 LISTENING

A **Use background knowledge.** Read the sentences below. What does the word in bold mean? When do election campaigns typically happen?

There are two candidates running for mayor. The **campaign** will begin on February 1st, and the election will be on March 15th.

B 🔊 **Listen for gist.** Listen to the beginning of speeches given by Doris and Amelia. Choose the best answer to complete each sentence. (One answer is extra.) **CD 2 Track 15**

1. Doris is giving her speech because _____

2. Amelia is giving her speech because _____

    a. she is going to run for mayor.

    b. she has been elected mayor.

    c. she has lost the race for mayor.

C 🔊 **Listen for context.** Listen again. Choose the best answers. **CD 2 Track 15**

1. When Doris says *never in my wildest dreams*, she means...

    a. she was pretty sure.

    b. she couldn't imagine it.

2. When Doris says *I gave it my best shot*, she means...

    a. she was very disappointed.

    b. she worked really hard.

3. When Amelia says *Doris and I were running neck and neck*, she means...

    a. they had almost the same number of votes.

    b. there was a clear winner.

4. When Amelia says *we saw a record turnout*, she means...

    a. a large number of people voted.

    b. a small number of people voted.

D 🔊 🔁 **Listen for main ideas.** Now listen to the rest of Amelia's speech. Check (✓) the topics she refers to in her speech. What key words in the listening helped you choose your answers? Tell a partner. **CD 2 Track 16**

☐ the economy   ☐ public transportation   ☐ crime   ☐ pollution   ☐ education

E 🔁 Look at the topics in **D**. Which one do you think is the biggest problem where you live? Why? Tell a partner.

Pollution is a major problem for many cities.

4 SPEAKING

A 🔊 Listen to and read the speech below. What is the problem? What is one thing causing it? Can you think of other causes? **CD 2 Track 17**

Today I'd like to talk to you about rush hour traffic. I'll begin by telling you about the problem. Then I'll list the three things I think are causing this problem.

So, let's start by talking about rush hour traffic in this city. We've all experienced it, and in recent years it's gotten worse. Ten years ago, it used to take about 45 minutes to drive across town. Now it takes two hours. One of the main causes of this problem is too many cars on the road. More cars means more traffic and, of course, more traffic accidents. Another cause of rush hour traffic is...

B 🔊 **Pronunciation: Using pauses in public speaking.** Read the sentences below. Guess where the speaker will pause. Write a slash mark (/) for each pause. Then listen and check your answers. **CD 2 Track 18**

What is one of the biggest problems facing our city today? It's rush hour traffic.

Today we're going to talk about this important problem. I'll begin by telling you about the problem. Then I'll list three things…

C 🔊 🔁 Listen again to the speech in **A** and take turns saying it aloud with a partner. Pay attention to pausing. **CD 2 Track 17**

SPEAKING STRATEGY

D Match each word on the left with one on the right to make a list of common city problems. Write them on a piece of paper. Can you add to the list?

unaffordable	high		streets	unemployment
dirty	noise		housing	pollution

E 🔁 Choose one of the city problems in **D** or one of your own. Work with a partner and complete the information below.

Problem: _____

Causes of the problem:

1. _____

2. _____

3. _____

Useful Expressions: Language for presentations
Stating the purpose
Today, I'd like to talk to you about...
I'll begin by (talking about the issue). / I'll provide an overview of (the issue).
Then I'll list the (two / three / four)...
Stating important points
Let's talk first about... / Let's start by talking about...
One of the main causes of (traffic) is...
Another / A second cause of (traffic) is...
And finally...

F 👥 Join another pair and follow the instructions. Then switch roles and repeat.

Presenters: Use the Useful Expressions to explain your problem in **E** clearly. One person should introduce the talk. The second person should explain the causes of the problem.

Listeners: Take notes. After the presentation, give suggestions for how to solve the problem.

5 GRAMMAR

A Turn to page 210. Complete the exercises. Then do **B–D** below.

Too + Adjective / Adverb; *too much* / *too many* + Noun				
	too	Adjective / adverb	(Infinitive)	
You're 17. You're	**too**	young	to vote.	
I can't understand him. He speaks	**too**	quickly.		
	too much / *too many*	Noun	(Infinitive)	
	Too much	pollution		is bad for your lungs.
Our city has	**too many**	problems	to solve	in one day.

Adjective / Adverb + *enough*; *enough* + Noun				
	Adjective / adverb	*enough*	(Infinitive)	
I'm 21. I'm	old	**enough**	to vote.	
These are good seats. I can hear	well	**enough**.		
	enough	Noun	(Infinitive)	
We have	**enough**	water	to get by	for now.
They have	**enough**	police officers		on the street.

B Complete the statements about school life with *too*, *too much*, *too many*, and *enough*.

School Life	Agree	Disagree
1. There are _____ rules in this school.	☐	☐
2. There is _____ emphasis on memorization.	☐	☐
3. We don't have _____ time for extracurricular activities.	☐	☐
4. Classes are not interesting _____.	☐	☐
5. _____ students study only to pass the test.	☐	☐
6. We don't have _____ opportunities to practice English conversation.	☐	☐
7. There's _____ homework.	☐	☐
8. The school day is _____ long.	☐	☐

C Now check (✓) *Agree* or *Disagree* for each statement in **B**.

> I think there are too many rules in this school. For example, we shouldn't have to wear school uniforms all the time.

D 🔁 Share your answers with a partner. Give examples and discuss solutions for the statements you agreed with.

> I agree. I think you can look neat enough in a pair of jeans and a nice shirt.

6 COMMUNICATION

A Follow the instructions to complete the survey below. Then check (✓) *Yes* or *No*.

- **For questions 1–6:** Write *enough* before or after each word. (Only one position is correct.)
- **For questions 7–12:** Write *too*, *too much*, or *too many*.

	Yes	**No**

1. Did you get _____ sleep _____ last night?

2. Do you have _____ credits _____ to graduate?

3. Is it _____ quiet _____ for you to study at home?

4. Do you typically have _____ time _____ to finish your homework?

5. Have you eaten _____ food _____ today?

6. Do you get along _____ well _____ with your parents?

7. Do you spend _____ time watching TV?

8. Is English _____ difficult to learn?

9. Do you sometimes eat _____ sweets?

10. Do you have _____ problems in your life?

11. Is it possible to earn _____ money?

12. At 20, are people _____ young to get married?

B [icon] Use the questions in **A** to interview a partner. Ask follow-up questions.

> Is it quiet enough for you to study at home?

> No, not really. It's pretty noisy.

> Where do you study then?

> Mostly at the library.

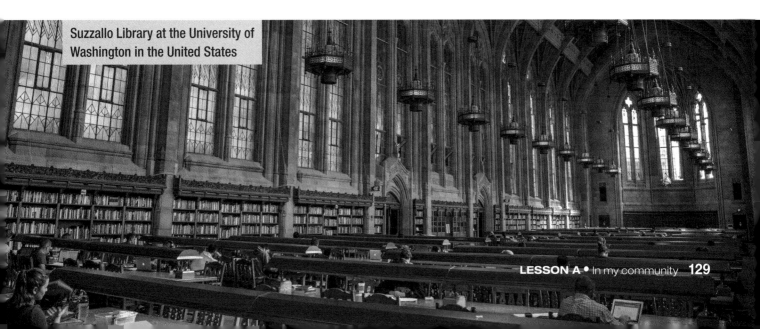

Suzzallo Library at the University of Washington in the United States

Sydney, Australia, has so much urban sprawl that the city has spread almost into the ocean!

1 VOCABULARY

A Read about the problem of sprawl. Then tell a partner: Is sprawl a problem in your area?

- Sprawl is a problem in my city. In the past five years, there has been a lot of new **development**. As this **spreads** across the land, it **destroys** parks, farms, and open spaces.

- In many of these new neighborhoods, people live far away from public transportation, stores, and schools. This **forces** people to **rely on** their cars so they can drive longer distances. Driving a lot is a **waste** of time. It also creates more pollution.

- So what can we do? First, we should stop all new development. This will **protect** our open spaces for future generations. Then, we should **support** a law that **provides** money for public transportation and new bike paths. This will **encourage** people to leave their cars at home. If this happens, air quality will **improve**.

B Write a blue word from **A** next to its definition.

1. ___encourage___: to persuade or get someone to do something

2. _____: to damage completely

3. _____: to keep something safe

4. _____: to move gradually outward

5. _____: to use something in a bad or careless way

6. _____: to try to help a person or idea succeed

7. _____: to offer or give something

8. _____: to make someone do something difficult

9. _____: the building of houses, stores, and other structures

10. _____: to need or depend on something

11. _____: to make better

C Answer the questions with your partner using the new words in **A**.

1. What is the problem with sprawl? What does it do?

2. What does the writer suggest doing? How will these things help?

2 LISTENING

A 🔄 Look at the photos. Do you live in an urban or suburban area? Explain to a partner.

urban

suburban

B 🔊 **Listen for details; Infer information.** You will hear three speakers. Where do they live now? Where do they want to live in the future? Write *U* for urban and *S* for suburban. Write *NM* if the information is not mentioned. **CD 2 Track 19**

Bella: now: _____   Anne: now: _____   Mercedes: now: _____

     future: _____   future: _____   future: _____

C 🔊 **Listen for reasons.** Where does each person want to live? Circle the answers below. Then listen and take notes on their reasons. **CD 2 Track 20**

1. Bella wants to live in the city / suburbs.   Reason(s): _____
2. Anne wants to live in the city / suburbs.   Reason(s): _____
3. Mercedes wants to live in the city / suburbs.   Reason(s): _____

D 🔄 What do you think the underlined expressions mean? Which person from **B** do you think would say each sentence? Write the names. Explain your answers to a partner.

1. I hope I can move—I have to <u>wait and see</u>, I guess.   _____
2. Now that I've <u>put down roots</u>, I probably won't move.   _____
3. I needed <u>a change of scenery</u>, and I got it!   _____

E 🔄 Where do you want to live in the future? Why? Tell a partner.

3 READING

A 🔁 **Use background knowledge.** This article is about a *daycare center* and a *retirement home*. What are these places? How are they similar? Discuss with a partner.

B 🔁 **Make predictions; Infer information.** Look at the photo. Answer the questions with a partner.

1. How do you think the people in the photo know each other?

2. Look at the word *intergenerational* in the caption. What do you think it means?

C **Infer meaning.** Read the article. Then match the words (1–4) with the correct definitions (a–d).

1. at risk (line 4) _____

2. launched (line 11) _____

3. be exposed to (line 31–32) _____

4. tolerant (line 34) _____

a. started

b. in danger of something bad happening

c. be given the chance to experience something new

d. able to accept different ideas and situations

D 🔁 **Read for details; Draw conclusions.** The article talks about an intergenerational program. What are the benefits of the program? Underline them in the passage. Can you think of any challenges? Explain your ideas to a partner.

E 🔁 Why do you think many older and younger people are in retirement homes and daycare centers in the US? Is this common in your country? Do you think it's good? Why or why not? Discuss with a partner.

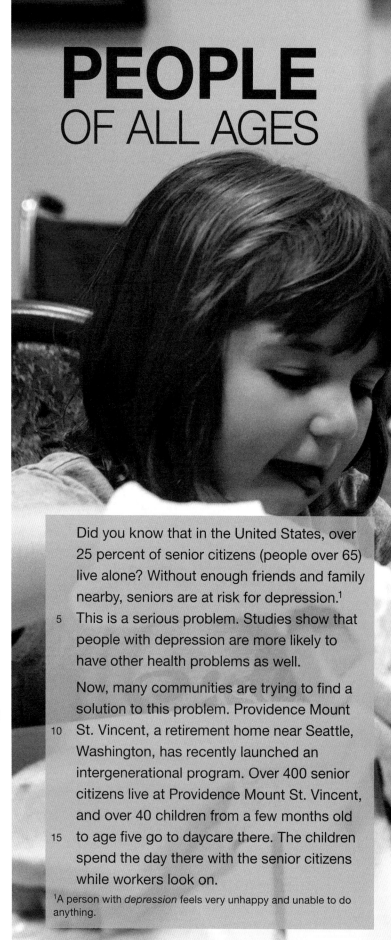

PEOPLE
OF ALL AGES

Did you know that in the United States, over 25 percent of senior citizens (people over 65) live alone? Without enough friends and family nearby, seniors are at risk for depression.[1]

5 This is a serious problem. Studies show that people with depression are more likely to have other health problems as well.

Now, many communities are trying to find a solution to this problem. Providence Mount
10 St. Vincent, a retirement home near Seattle, Washington, has recently launched an intergenerational program. Over 400 senior citizens live at Providence Mount St. Vincent, and over 40 children from a few months old
15 to age five go to daycare there. The children spend the day there with the senior citizens while workers look on.

[1] A person with *depression* feels very unhappy and unable to do anything.

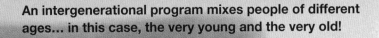

An intergenerational program mixes people of different ages… in this case, the very young and the very old!

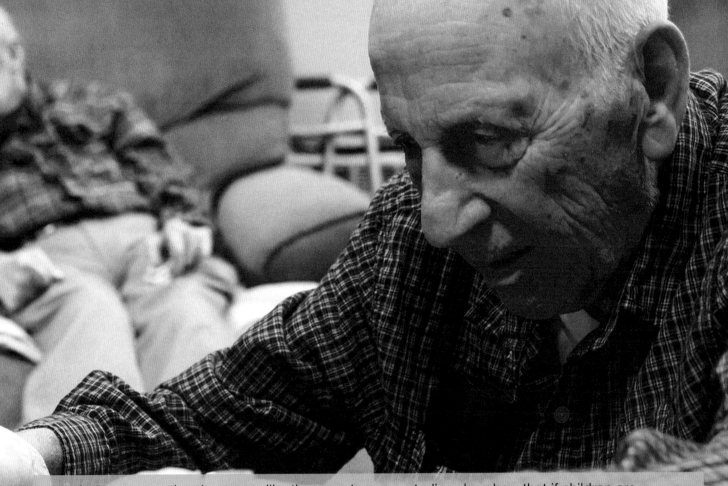

An intergenerational program like the one at Providence Mount St. Vincent has clear
20 benefits. For the older people, their social life improves; they read to and play games with the children and encourage them in a wide range of other activities. Being involved with the children makes the seniors feel useful and
25 happy, and if they feel happy, their overall mental and physical health may improve.

The children also benefit from the program. They have an enthusiastic and patient group of people to play with in a safe environment.
30 Some of the seniors are also disabled,[2] and

studies also show that if children are exposed to people with disabilities at a young age, they will learn to be more tolerant and understanding of people
35 like this.

Providence Mount St. Vincent was even featured in a documentary film called *Present Perfect*. As families of both the young and the old see the benefits, intergenerational
40 programs are expanding. The film's message is starting to spread: even if the very young and the very old don't have a shared past or future, their shared present can be perfect.

[2] A *disabled* person has an illness or injury that makes doing certain physical or mental activities (like walking or thinking) difficult.

4 GRAMMAR

A Turn to page 211. Complete the exercises. Then do **B–D** below.

Future Real Conditionals	
If clause	**Result clause**
If a woman **works**, If we **don't protect** our open spaces,	(then) a family **will have** more money.* (then) future generations **won't have** places to relax.
Result clause	**If clause**
A family **will have** more money	if a woman **works**.

*If you aren't certain, you can use *might (not)* or *may (not)* in a result clause:
*If a woman works, a family **may / might have** more money.*

B 🔁 Complete the sentences with a partner. How many sentences can you make? Make follow-up sentences for each one.

> If people have smaller families,…

> If you eat too many sweets,…

> If you eat too many sweets, you'll probably get sick.

> And if you get sick, you might miss class.

C Take out five small pieces of paper. On each piece, write an *if* clause like the examples in **B**.

D 👥 Work in a small group. Follow the steps below.

1. Put all your papers together and mix them. Put them face down on the desk in a pile.

2. One person begins. Turn over a paper. You have 15 seconds to complete the sentence.
   - If you make a correct sentence, you get a point. Then put the paper aside.
   - If you don't make a correct sentence, put the paper at the bottom of the pile.

3. Then the next person goes. Play until you use all the papers. Who got the most points?

5 WRITING

A Read the paragraph. What is the writer predicting? Under the paragraph, circle your opinion.

> In the future, robots will do more of our jobs. Robots already work in some places today, like factories and restaurants. In five to ten years, you may see them in hospitals and schools. They'll even drive cars. Will this improve our lives?

In my opinion, it will / won't.

B Complete the outline below with ideas to support your answer choice in **A**.

If robots do more of our jobs, what will happen? Why is this good or bad?

_____

If the above happens, what will happen?

_____

If that happens, what will happen?

_____

For these reasons, I think robots doing more of our jobs will / won't improve our lives.

C Write a paragraph with your opinion. Begin by writing the paragraph in **A**. Then continue your paragraph using your ideas from the outline in **B**.

D 🔁 Exchange your writing with a partner. Read his or her paragraph.

1. Are there any mistakes? If yes, circle them.

2. What is your partner's opinion and what reasons does he or she give? Do you agree?

3. Return the paper to your partner. Make corrections to your own paragraph.

In your outline, think about how one event affects another: If A happens, then B might happen. If B happens, then C might happen.

6 COMMUNICATION

A Read each problem and suggest solutions for each one. Add your own ideas, too.

Problem: Too many young people are leaving rural areas and moving to big cities.

Suggestions:

1. _Give people money to encourage them to stay in their hometowns._

2. _Ask companies to provide_ _____

Problem: There's too much suburban development, and this is causing sprawl.

Suggestions:

1. _Limit the number of new homes being built each month._ _____

2. _Support a law to_ _____

B Imagine you are running for political office. Prepare a short speech. Explain what you'll do to solve the problems in **A**.

C 👥 Work in a group of four people. Follow the steps below.

1. **Students A & B:** Give your speeches to the group.

   Students C & D: Listen and take notes. At the end, decide: Whose speech was better? Why?

2. Change roles and repeat step 1.

> Too many young people are leaving our area and moving to the city for jobs. If I get elected, I'll...

1 STORYBOARD

A Mr. Stevens and his son, Ian, are waiting in the doctor's office. Look at the pictures and complete the conversations. More than one answer is possible for each blank.

1 Excuse me. Can I _____ to you for a moment?

Sure, go ahead.

My son is sick. _____ waiting for over an hour to see the doctor.

2 Please _____ a minute. Let me check with the doctor.

3 Five minutes later

CLINIC

Mr. Stevens and Ian? The doctor is _____ to see you now.

4 Hi, Ian. So, _____ _____?

I'm _____. I _____ a fever, and I _____ shivering.

5 After the exam

In my opinion, Ian should _____ _____.

OK.

6 Thank _____ so much.

I'm glad I could help.

B 👥 Practice the conversations in groups of four. Then change roles and practice again.

C 🔄 With a partner, create and perform your own conversation between a doctor and a patient.

2 SEE IT AND SAY IT

A 🔄 Look at the picture. Use the words in the box to talk about it. Then answer the questions with a partner.

campaign	election	speech
candidate	enthusiastic	term
citizens	running for (a political office)	

- Is this Mr. Gold's first political campaign?
- Look at the banner. Which of these ideas does Mr. Gold support?

  building more schools   encouraging public transportation

  raising taxes   stopping business development

- Who do you think will vote for Mike Gold? Who is going to vote against him?

B 🔲 Work with a partner. Write a brief speech for Mike Gold. Perform your speech for another pair.

C 🔲 Work with a partner. Write a brief speech for a candidate running against Mike Gold. Perform your speech for another pair.

3 I'M EXHAUSTED BECAUSE...

A 🔄 Match Camille's behaviors on the left with the causes on the right. Compare your answers with a partner's.

1. Camille is stressed out.
2. She's dizzy and hungry.
3. She's breathing hard.
4. She's shivering.
5. She's just swallowed two aspirin.

a. She's been playing tennis for two hours.
b. She forgot to bring her coat.
c. She works too much.
d. She skipped breakfast and lunch.
e. She has a headache.

B In two to three minutes, add as many items as you can to each category.

Things that make you...

1. cough: _cigarette smoke,_ _____
2. feel exhausted: _____
3. feel dizzy: _____
4. shiver: _____

C 🔄 Ask a partner questions beginning with *What makes you...?* for each category in **B**.

4 TERRY'S DIARY

A Use the words in the box to complete Terry's diary entry about living in the city. (Three words are extra.)

action	opportunities
active	pollution
activity	taxes
affordable	traffic
dirty	transportation
in	with

Last night I went out with some old friends. They're all married and live in the suburbs. I'm single and still live in the city. They wanted to know why I still live here.

It's true—living in the city can be annoying sometimes. We have a problem with (1.) _____ streets. Plus, there's a lack of (2.) _____ housing. Everything is so expensive! The air (3.) _____ is pretty bad, too. You have to deal (4.) _____ a lot of these kinds of hassles every day.

On the other hand, the city is pretty great! First of all, there are a lot of job (5.) _____ here. I certainly have a well-paying job! The (6.) _____ can be pretty bad, but I avoid it. I take public (7.) _____ everywhere. I also stay (8.) _____ by walking all over the city.

The city is where all the (9.) _____ is, and I love it here!

B 🔄 What kind of hassles (difficult or frustrating situations) do you have to deal with in your city or town? Make a list with a partner.

5 POKER TIPS

A Read the advice given by a professional about how to play poker well. Rewrite each tip in reported speech, using the verb in parentheses.

1. Learn the different kinds of cards. (tell)

   _____

2. Don't bet too much money. (ask)

   _____

3. Study the other players' facial expressions. (ask)

   _____

4. Don't take unnecessary risks. (tell)

   _____

B Now think of a sport or game that you know how to play. Complete the sentences below. Don't show anyone!

People: There are... people on each team. / You play by yourself.

Equipment: The game is played with...

Location: It's played in / on...

Playing the game: The game starts when...

How to win: The object of the game is...

C 🔁 With a partner, take turns asking and answering questions about each other's sport or game. Can you guess what it is?

> Is it a sport?

> No. It's a card game.

> How many people play it?

> Four to six people play it. There aren't any teams—you play by yourself.

6 LISTENING

A 🔊 You are going to hear a lecture. Complete the notes. Write no more than two words for each answer. Then answer the question below.
CD 2 Track 22

In which class would you probably hear this lecture?

☐ science
☐ math
☐ business

I. Dehydration: defined

A. Most of your body's weight is due to _____ —about _____%.

B. Dehydration occurs when the amount of water _____ the body is greater than the amount _____.

   1. "I'm dehydrated" means _____.

II. Causes

A. You can become dehydrated when you _____ a lot or are _____ on a hot day.

III. Symptoms

A. Include a _____ and getting _____.

   1. If you remain dehydrated, you may have to go to the _____.

Look at the photo. Answer the questions.

1 What store were the women shopping in?

2 How much do you think it costs to shop there?

3 Where do you like to spend money?

UNIT GOALS

1 Describe your saving and spending habits

2 Make and accept apologies

3 Express hopes and regrets using *wish*

4 Talk about things you do with money

Women in a shopping area in Ho Chi Minh City, Vietnam

If you saw someone in a city like this giving away an item for free, what would you do? Would you trust them?

1 VIDEO Take the Money... and Run?

A ▶ 🔄 Watch the first 45 seconds of the video. Fill in the blanks. Explain the experiment to a partner.

1. They set up a _____.

2. They are offering free _____.

3. People can _____ as much or as little as they want.

4. Hidden _____ are everywhere.

5. What will people do? Will they take any _____?

B 🔄 What do you think the people in the experiment will do? Why do you think that? Tell a partner.

C ▶ Now watch the full video. Right before each person makes a decision, make your prediction. Then watch and check your answer.

Will the person take it? If your answer is *yes*, how much will he or she take (a little or a lot)?

1. first young woman ☐ no ☐ yes │ ☐ a little ☐ a lot

2. older man ☐ no ☐ yes │ ☐ a little ☐ a lot

3. young man ☐ no ☐ yes │ ☐ a little ☐ a lot

D ▶ ⚙ Watch the end of the video. What do you think happens when they remove the man from the booth? How will the results of the experiment change? Discuss in a small group.

2 VOCABULARY

A Read the money quiz and review the items in **blue**. Then take the quiz.

1. a. I **make a budget** and **stick to it**.
   b. I don't **have a budget**, but I want to try to make one.
   c. Budget? What budget?

2. a. I should **save** more **money**, but I never seem to do it.
   b. I sometimes save a little, but then I always spend it.
   c. Saving money is easy for me because I have a goal in mind.

3. a. I try not to **borrow money** because it's always hard to **pay** it **back**.
   b. I sometimes borrow money even though I don't like to **go into debt**.
   c. I borrow money when I need to.

4. a. When I **lend money**, I don't worry about people **owing** me.
   b. People don't usually ask me for money.
   c. I can't **afford** to lend anyone money. I'm too **broke**.

5. a. I can **get by** on very little money. I'm used to it.
   b. When I'm **short on cash**, I don't go shopping or out to eat.
   c. I need a certain amount of money to live well.

Word Bank
Things we do with money
stick to / **make** / **have** a budget
save ↔ **spend** money
borrow ↔ **lend** money

B 🔁 Share your answers with a partner. Ask and answer follow-up questions.

> Saving money is easy for me because I have a goal in mind.

> Really? What goal is that?

Many countries put images that are important to them on their money. South Africa's money has images of the country's famous wildlife.

3 LISTENING

A  **Use background knowledge.** We all have basic needs in our lives. Look at the pictures below. What basic needs are they? What other basic needs can you think of? Discuss with a partner.

BASIC NEEDS OF LIFE

> One basic need is water. Everyone needs drinking water.

B 🔊 **Listen for details.** You are going to hear a short talk. First, listen to the introduction and fill in the missing words. **CD 2 Track 23**

Let me ask you a question: Can _____ buy _____? That is, if you have *more* _____, will you be _____? What do you think?

C 🔊 **Take notes.** Now listen to the full talk. Complete the outline with the missing words. **CD 2 Track 24**

1. The Smith family now
   a. _____ children
   b. barely _____ by
   c. worry about _____ and _____

2. Basic needs—the things you need to survive
   a. a _____ place to live
   b. enough _____ to eat
   c. a way to make _____

3. The Smith family after receiving money
   a. they are _____ worried
   b. they can pay their _____
   c. they have less _____

D  **Summarize.** With a partner, use the outline in **C** to summarize the talk you heard.

> The speaker talks about the Smith family. They have four children...

WORLD LINK

Where are the happiest people in the world? Go online and find out. Were you surprised by the answer?

144 UNIT 10 • Money

4 SPEAKING

A 🔊 Mike got takeout from a nearby restaurant. Listen to and read the conversation. Underline the two apologies. How do Eva and Mike respond to the apologies? Circle their responses. **CD 2 Track 25**

EVA: Thanks for picking up lunch, Mike.

MIKE: Sure.

EVA: How much do I owe you?

MIKE: Your total comes to $10.20. You can just give me ten dollars.

EVA: OK. Oh, wait.... Sorry, I've only got a 20-dollar bill. I wish I had something smaller....

MIKE: Don't worry about it. Why don't we eat first and then you can pay me later?

EVA: Oh, OK. Thanks.

MIKE: No problem. OK, here you go: A hamburger and fries for me—and a turkey sandwich for you.

EVA: Um, where's my soda?

MIKE: Oh, no! I forgot your soda. Sorry... my mistake.

EVA: No problem. It happens. I'll just have water instead.

B 🔁 Practice the conversation with a partner.

SPEAKING STRATEGY

C Look at each situation. What happened in each one?

D 🔁 Imagine that you are one of the people in **C**. With a partner, use the Useful Expressions to apologize and accept the apology. Then switch roles and repeat with the other situation.

Useful Expressions: Apologizing		Useful Expressions: Accepting an apology
Small accident or mistake	**Serious accident or mistake**	Don't worry about it.
I'm sorry. It was an accident.	I'm really sorry that I forgot to...	Oh, that's OK.
Sorry. My mistake.	I'm so sorry about damaging...	No problem. It happens.
I can't believe I did that.	I want to apologize for what happened.	Apology accepted.

5 GRAMMAR

A Turn to page 212. Complete the exercises. Then do **B**–**E** below.

Wish Statements		
Present situation		**Wish statement**
He **won't** pay me back.	will → would	I **wish** (that) he **would** pay me back.
I **can't** lend you any money.	can → could	I **wish** (that) I **could** lend you some money.
I **am** not good at saving money.	am → were*	I **wish** (that) I **were** good at saving money.
She doesn't **have** a budget.	have → had	She **wishes** (that) she **had** a budget.

Were is considered more correct than *was* in *wish* statements with *be*.

To express impossible or unlikely wishes about present situations, use a *wish* statement. The verb following *wish* is in the past.

B Read each situation. Then write a *wish* statement for each one.

1. I'm not famous.

   _____

2. I'm broke.

   _____

3. I have to work on the weekend.

   _____

4. I can't pay you back.

   _____

5. I can't afford to pay my credit card bill.

   _____

6. I have gone into debt.

   _____

C  Choose one of the situations in **B** and make a short conversation. Practice it with a partner.

Student A: You are upset about a situation.

Student B: Listen to Student A and try to help.

B: Hey, what's wrong?

A: I have to work this weekend.

B: Really? That's terrible.

A: I know. I wish I didn't have to.

B: Why do you have to work?

A: I have to make some money. I've been spending too much lately and…

D Pick another situation from **B** and make another conversation. This time, switch roles when you practice it.

E Choose one of your conversations and perform it for the class.

In many cultures, there are traditional ways to make a wish, like throwing a coin in a *wishing well*.

6 COMMUNICATION

A 🗣️ Work with a partner. Read the information below. Look up any words you don't know in a dictionary.

APARTMENTS FOR RENT!
Come and spend your summer by the beach

Room with a view!	Fun in the sun!
About this apartment	**About this apartment**
Ten years old	Brand-new apartment
2 bedrooms, 1 bath	Fold-out sofa bed sleeps two
Big balcony facing the beach	Very close to the beach
No noise allowed after 10 PM	No air conditioner
2 nights minimum stay	1 week minimum stay
7 nights maximum stay	3 weeks maximum stay
$200 per night for first three nights; $150 for each additional night	$150 per night
The local area	**The local area**
There are no restaurants, but there is a convenience store nearby.	There are two restaurants nearby that serve dinner.
There is a washer and a dryer in the apartment.	There is a laundromat down the street.
Transportation	**Transportation**
5-minute walk to the train station	20-minute bus ride to the train station
1 hour to the city center by train	20 minutes to the city center by train

B 🗣️ Now imagine that you and your partner are going to rent one of these apartments for a summer vacation. Which one will you choose? Discuss what you like and don't like about each one. Then choose one.

Things to consider:

- You are both students, so you are on a budget. You don't want to spend too much money.

- On the other hand, money isn't everything! You also want to have fun.

- Your vacation is going to be from three to seven nights long.

> I like the first one, but I wish it were closer to the city center.

C 👥 Take a vote as a class. Which apartment was more popular? Why?

LESSON B   STRIKING IT RICH

1 VOCABULARY

A 🔁 Have you, or someone you know, ever won anything in the lottery? Tell a partner.

B Read the question and answers in the box. Write each item in **blue** next to its definition.

1. give to charity: _____

2. make a lot of money suddenly: _____

3. save: _____

4. money you've made: _____

5. waste: _____

6. use money to make more money: _____

C 🔁 Answer the question in the box. Explain your answer(s) to a partner.

> I would set aside some of the money. It's always
> good to save money. Then I'd buy a car!

Imagine you strike it rich in the lottery. What would you do with the money?

a. I'd **donate** some to a charity (an organization that helps others).

b. I'd **invest** some in a house.

c. I'd **set aside** some of the **earnings** for the future.

d. I'd probably **squander** the money on things like expensive cars and vacations.

Word Bank
Word partnerships with *money*
donate
earn / make
invest
set aside / save ↔ spend
squander / waste

148 **UNIT 10** • Money

2 LISTENING

A 🔄 **Use background knowledge.** Name a famous millionaire. How did the person make his or her money? Discuss with a partner.

B **Make predictions.** Read the information below and then guess the answers to 1–3.

> Two researchers studied wealthy people. They wrote about their findings in a book called *The Millionaire Next Door.* Here are some things they learned.

Most millionaires…

1. wear expensive clothes.	True	False
2. drive expensive cars.	True	False
3. donate some of their money.	True	False

Word Bank

affordable = not expensive

millionaire = a person with at least a million dollars

wealthy = rich

C 🔊 **Check predictions.** Listen to the interview and check your answers in **B**. Correct the false statements. **CD 2 Track 26**

D 🔊 **Listen for details.** What do you remember? Complete the sentences. Then listen and check your answers. **CD 2 Track 26**

ℹ️ Notice how the man speaking uses (*but*) *actually* and *but in fact* to show the opposite of what people think.

Most millionaires…

1. don't squander their money on expensive _____ or _____.

2. _____ their earnings in things like property.

3. make an annual _____ and don't _____ more money than they _____.

4. _____ some of their money for the future.

E 🔄 Answer the questions with a partner.

1. How did your idea of a typical millionaire in **B** compare to the speaker's?

2. Do you do any of the things in **D**? Which ones?

> I thought most millionaires…, but actually, they…

3 READING

A  **Make predictions.** Look at the pictures and the title of the article. How do you think these two groups have made money? Tell a partner.

B **Read for details.** Read and answer the questions about your people only. Write your answers on a piece of paper.

Student A: Read about the San.

Student B: Read about the monks.

1. Where do they live?

2. How do they make their money (or how will they in the future)?

3. How do they spend their money (or how will they in the future)?

C Ask your partner the questions in **B** about his or her people. Take notes. Then read the other profile to check your partner's answers.

D **Infer meaning.** Find the words in **bold** in the reading. Complete each sentence with the correct word(s).

1. If something is *worth money*, it is / isn't valuable.

2. You get *easy money* by working hard / without working at all.

3. If money *pours in*, it comes to you quickly / slowly.

4. If you *accept* something, you take it from / give it to another person.

E **Compare and evaluate.** Answer the questions with a partner. Use your notes to help you.

1. Are the San and the monks similar in any way?

2. Think about the ways the San and the monks are making money. Do you think it is good for them to earn money this way? Why or why not?

MONEY
FROM UNUSUAL
SOURCES

Greek monks

When you think of a monk, you might think of a quiet man living in a place far away from others. The "free monks" of Greece do live far from others, but they are anything but quiet. In fact, they sing. They have been recording songs and selling many albums in Greece.

People of all ages love them. Their songs are recorded in different styles (digital keyboard and rock, for example) and are not only religious. The monks also sing about problems like drugs and globalization.

The cash from music sales isn't **pouring in,** but the monks are earning some money. A few people don't like this; they think monks shouldn't sing for money. But the monks happily **accept** the money. They set it aside for summer camps for teenagers. The monks also donate some of the money to social programs that help many people.

The San people have lived in Southern Africa for almost 40,000 years, hunting[1] animals and gathering plants. But recently, many San people lost their land. Some tried to move to large cities, but it was hard to get jobs. Broke, they returned home and watched as their culture and traditions began to die.

But all this may be changing. The San have struck it rich. They recently signed an agreement with a large drug company. The San have traditional knowledge about plants that is **worth** a lot of **money.** The drug company is especially interested in a particular plant and how the San use it.

In the past, the San went on long hunting trips. While away from home, they ate a special plant to slow their hunger. Using the San's knowledge, the drug company wants to make a new medicine from this plant. For people around the world who have weight problems, this drug could really help.

The San are being careful with this "**easy money.**" They plan to use it to create jobs for their people. They also want to focus on education. Through education, they hope to save their culture and language for future generations.

[1]If you *hunt* an animal, you follow and kill it for food.

Southern Africa's San people

4 GRAMMAR

A Turn to page 213 and complete the exercises. Then do **B–D** below.

Negative Modals	
Impossibility	You **can't** have the winning lottery ticket. I have it!
Ability	Sorry, but I **can't** lend you any money. I'm broke.
Necessity	You **don't have to** / **don't need to** be rich to travel.
Advice	You **shouldn't** waste money on expensive cars.
Strong advice	You'**d better not** lose this ring. It's very valuable.

B 🔊 **Pronunciation: Word final /t/ and /d/.** Listen and repeat. Pay attention to the final /t/ and /d/ sounds. **CD 2 Track 28**

1. can'**t**   You can'**t** have the winning ticket.

2. don'**t**   You don'**t** have to be rich.

3. shouldn'**t**   You shouldn'**t** waste money.

4. You'**d** better no**t**   You'**d** better no**t** lose this ring.

C Complete the sentences with the negative form of each modal.

1. Money (can) _____ buy happiness.

2. You (should) _____ borrow money from friends.

3. You (have to) _____ go to college to get a good job.

4. You (had better) _____ show your wallet on the subway. Someone might steal it.

5. You (need to) _____ work for a large company to earn good money.

6. You (should) _____ pay for most things with a credit card.

7. You (can) _____ get married until you have a good job.

D 🔁 Say each sentence in **C** aloud. Pay attention to your pronunciation. Do you agree or disagree with each statement? Why? Tell a partner.

> You shouldn't pay for most things with a credit card.

> I agree. It's easy to spend too much money and go broke.

5 WRITING

A 🔁 Read the question below and one person's reply on the right. What reason does the writer give for his opinion? Can you think of one more reason? Tell a partner.

> A millionaire in your community plans to donate money to one group below. Which one should get the money and why? Give two reasons.
>
> - A charity: It helps poor teenagers go to college.
> - A museum: It needs the money or it will close.
> - A hospital: It helps people with cancer.

> In my opinion, the millionaire should donate money to the hospital for two important reasons. **For one thing**, everyone needs a hospital. People don't have to go to museums, and they don't need to go to college. But a person with cancer has to go to a hospital. With the money, the hospital can help more people. **In addition**...

B What do you think? Outline your ideas and then write a paragraph. Think of two reasons one group should get the money and the others shouldn't. Explain each reason in a sentence or two as shown in the example.

In my opinion, the millionaire should donate money to the

_____.

For one thing, _____.

In addition, _____.

For these reasons, I believe the millionaire should donate money to the

_____.

C 🔁 Exchange your writing with a partner. Circle any mistakes. Then return the paper to your partner. Make corrections to your own paragraph.

6 COMMUNICATION

A 👥 Work in a group of four. Each person should take a role. Students A, B, and C should think of two reasons he or she should get the money. Student D should think of questions to ask the others.

Student A: You work for the charity.

Student B: You work for the museum.

Student C: You work for the hospital.

Student D: You're the millionaire.

B 👥 Have a debate.

1. Each student (A, B, C) speaks for one minute. The others take notes.
2. At the end of each student's talk, Student D can ask questions.
3. After all three students have spoken, each student (A, B, C) has one minute to speak and argue against the other ideas.
4. At the end, Student D decides who gets the money and explains why.

> I work for the hospital. It does cancer research. We should get the money for two reasons. For one thing...

> You said "teenagers don't have to go to college." But a person has to go to college to get a good job!

11 HONESTY

Look at the photo. Answer the questions.

1 How do these two people feel?

2 What do you think happened before the photo was taken?

3 Have you ever been *lied to*? How did you feel?

UNIT GOALS

1 Speculate about imagined events

2 Give strong advice

3 Introduce surprising or opposing information

4 Report what someone else has said

Two men turn their backs to each other in Lombardy, Italy.

1 VIDEO Are You a Good Liar?

A You are going to do a simple test to see if you are a good liar or not. Follow the steps below.

1. Hold a small piece of paper to your forehead.
2. Take five seconds and write the capital letter *Q* on the paper.
3. Find a partner and compare your letters.

B Watch the video. Fill in the missing words.

Some people (1.) _____ the *Q* in a way that could be read by somebody (2.) _____ them, with the tail on the (3.) _____ side of their forehead. If you did that, then you tend to be aware of how other people (4.) _____ you. You are (5.) _____ being the center of attention and you are a (6.) _____ liar.

Other people (7.) _____ the *Q* so that they themselves can read it, with the tail on the (8.) _____ hand side of their forehead. If you did that, then you tend to be more of an introvert and (9.) _____ very good at lying.

C Discuss these questions with a partner.

1. What do you think of the results from the video? How did you draw your letter *Q*?
2. Do you think it's easy to spot a "good liar"? If so, how do you do it? If not, why not?

2 VOCABULARY

A  Look at the picture. Who are the people in it and what just happened? Do you think the boy is telling the truth? Why or why not? Tell a partner.

Word Bank

an honest person ↔ a liar

(depend on the) circumstances

exception

hurt (someone's feelings)

obvious

reward someone ↔ punish someone (for their behavior)

tell the truth ↔ tell a lie

B Read the statements below. Notice the words in **blue**. Look up any expressions you don't know. Then check (✓) the boxes that are true for you.

	Strongly agree	Agree	Disagree	Strongly disagree
1. Honesty is always best. There are no **exceptions** to this rule.				
2. You should never lie if it's **against the law**.				
3. You shouldn't **tell the truth** if it **hurts someone's feelings**.				
4. The truth isn't always so clear—it's not really **obvious**.				
5. Sometimes I tell the truth, and sometimes I don't. It depends on the **circumstances**.				
6. You shouldn't **punish** small children too severely if they **tell a lie**.				

C  Discuss your answers with a partner.

> I strongly agree that honesty is always best. If you always tell the truth, you won't have any trouble.

> I chose *disagree* for that one. I don't think you should *always* tell the truth.

3 LISTENING

A 🔁 **Use background knowledge.** You are going to hear a conversation about a job résumé. When you prepare a résumé, what kind of information should be included? Make a list with a partner.

_____   _____

_____   _____

B 🔊 **Listen for details.** Listen. Check (✓) *True* or *False*. Correct the false sentences to make them true. **CD 2 Track 29**

	True	False
1. Cindy quit her job.	☐	☐
2. Denise was sick last week.	☐	☐
3. There was a problem with Cindy's résumé.	☐	☐
4. She lied about her hours.	☐	☐
5. Denise is worried about the amount of work.	☐	☐
6. Interviewing is happening today.	☐	☐

C 🔊 Listen. Complete the expressions with the missing words. **CD 2 Track 30**

1. Well, _____, I don't know the details.

2. Uh-huh. She _____ her experience.

3. I agree. I don't think her boss was very happy that she had _____ him.

4. It's too bad but, _____, I'm worried.

D 🔊 🔁 **Pronunciation: Repeating with rising intonation to show surprise.** Listen. Speaker B shows surprise by repeating what Speaker A says. Notice the rising intonation and stress. Then practice the conversations with a partner. **CD 2 Track 31**

Conversation 1

A: Cindy was fired.

B: She was fired? Why?

A: Because she lied on her résumé.

B: I can't believe it!

Conversation 2

A: Cindy got into trouble.

B: She got into trouble? How?

A: She dented her parents' car.

B: You're kidding!

E 🔁 **Pronunciation: Repeating with rising intonation to show surprise.** Work with a partner. Use the situations below to make short conversations about Cindy like the ones in **D**. Remember to repeat with rising intonation to show surprise.

1. fail her exam / cheat on it

2. get a ticket / be caught speeding

3. move out / have an argument with her roommate

4 SPEAKING

A 🔊 Listen to and read the conversation. Where are Mr. and Mrs. Ward? What's the problem? **CD 2 Track 32**

MR. WARD: So, how's the chicken?

MRS. WARD: Delicious. How about your steak?

MR. WARD: It's all right...

MRS. WARD: Are you being honest? You don't sound very happy with it.

MR. WARD: Well, it's not cooked right. I asked for medium rare. This is well done.

MRS. WARD: Why don't you send it back?

MR. WARD: Oh, I don't want to bother anyone. I can eat it, I guess.

MRS. WARD: But it's expensive. I don't think you should eat it. Let's call the waiter. You won't hurt his feelings!

MR. WARD: Yeah, but...

MRS. WARD: If you don't say something, you're not going to enjoy your meal. Excuse me, waiter!

B 🔁 What would you say to the waiter? How would you complain? Write an ending to the conversation and practice it with a partner.

SPEAKING STRATEGY

C 🔁 Read about the three situations below. Choose one and write a role play with a partner.

Student A: Play the role of one of the friends or the coworker.

Student B: Warn Student A about his or her actions. Use the Useful Expressions to give strong opinions.

Useful Expressions: Giving strong advice
If you don't leave a bigger tip, the waiter **is going to** be upset.
I don't think you should spend so much time playing games on your computer.
You have to do your homework by yourself.

Your friend, who is a student in the US, often doesn't leave a big enough tip in restaurants.	Your coworker wastes a lot of time playing games on her computer.	Your friend, who doesn't like to study, often copies another friend's homework.

D 👥 Perform your dialog for the class.

5 GRAMMAR

A Turn to page 214. Complete the exercises. Then do **B–C** below.

Present Unreal Conditionals	
If clause	**Result clause**
If you **told** the truth,	(then) you **would feel** relieved.
If I **didn't have** a lot of homework,	(then) I**'d go** to the movies.
If I **found** a wallet,	(then) I**'d return** it.
Result clause	**If clause**
You**'d feel relieved**	if you **told** the truth.

Present unreal conditionals are used to talk about imagined or unreal events.
The *if* clause presents an imagined condition. It is not true right now.
The result clause presents an imagined result. It can come first or second in the sentence with no change in meaning.

B Use the correct form of the verb in parentheses to make present unreal conditional sentences.

1. If I (graduate) __*graduated*__ with honors, I (throw) __*would throw*__ a big party.

2. If today (be) _____ a holiday, I (stay) _____ at home.

3. If I (have) _____ a lot of time off, I (go) _____ to Colombia.

4. I (not / have) _____ time to see my friends if I (get) _____ a part-time job.

5. If I (not / study) _____ English, I (study) _____ German.

6. I (be) _____ good at basketball if I (be) _____ taller.

C Get into a group of four people. Follow the steps below. See how long you can go for. Then switch roles and start again.

Student A: Start a sentence chain. Choose one of the *if* clauses in **B** and finish the sentence with your own idea.

Student B: Add a sentence to Student A's sentence.

Students C & D: Continue the game with your own sentences.

> If today were a holiday, I'd go somewhere fun.

> If I went somewhere fun, I'd buy a souvenir.

> If I bought a souvenir, I'd give it to...

If you were in Istanbul, would you buy a lamp as a souvenir?

6 COMMUNICATION

A Look at the situations. Would you ever do any of these things? Write *yes*, *no*, or *maybe*.

Would you ever...

1. eat a whole platter of food at a party? _____

2. keep a pair of sunglasses that you found on the ground? _____

3. use the restroom in a cafe without actually buying anything there? _____

4. stand and read an entire magazine in a store without buying it? _____

5. download music, TV shows, or movies from the Internet without paying? _____

6. take extra supplies from your office to use at home? _____

B Discuss your answers in **A** with a partner.

> Would you ever keep a pair of sunglasses that you found on the street?

> It depends on the circumstances. If they were expensive, I'd probably keep them!

> **i** If you answered *yes*, you can use *definitely* in your answer. If you answered *maybe*, you might want to use *probably* in your answer.

When you need help, who do you count on?

1 VOCABULARY

A Match items 1–6 with their definitions from the box. Two items have the same definition.

a. dependable   d. relying on
b. honest   e. believe in
c. do what you   say you will do

1. _____ I can't do it myself. I'm **counting on** you to help.

2. _____ He's a **trustworthy** employee. He's never been late to work.

3. _____ A **truthful** person doesn't lie on a résumé.

4. _____ I promised to help you, and I'm going to **keep my word**.

5. _____ I'm sure she'll get the job. I **have confidence in** her.

6. _____ I **trust** you. I know that you are telling the truth.

B Take the quiz below.

1. Does a person have to be truthful to succeed?

   ☐ yes   ☐ no

2. Do you typically trust strangers?

   ☐ yes   ☐ no

3. Do you have confidence in yourself and your abilities?

   ☐ yes   ☐ no

4. Do you always keep your word?

   ☐ yes   ☐ no

5. Who do you usually count on to give good personal advice?

   _____

6. Who would you trust with a secret?

   _____

C 🔲 Interview a partner using the questions in **B**. Discuss your ideas.

> I think you have to be truthful to be successful.

> I agree. You can lie sometimes, but you shouldn't all the time.

2 LISTENING

A  What are some reasons that people lie? Make a list of ideas in your notebook with a partner.

B 🔊 **Identify key details.** Listen to the first part of a lecture. What are reasons people lie? List the two reasons you hear. Are either of these reasons on your list from **A**? **CD 2 Track 33**

Reasons people lie

1. _____

2. _____

C 🔊 **Infer meaning.** Read sentences 1–4. The speakers use the expressions in italics in the talk. Listen to the full lecture and choose the best answer. **CD 2 Track 34**

1. If someone tells you a *white lie*, they tell a lie to _____.

   a. hurt your feelings   b. be polite   c. make you laugh

2. If you *catch someone in a lie*, you _____.

   a. discover a person is lying   b. forgive a person for lying   c. tell someone a big lie

3. If you *hesitate* when you are talking, you speak in a _____ way.

   a. clear, direct   b. careful, honest   c. nervous, uncertain

4. A *dishonest* person _____ truthful.

   a. is   b. might be   c. is not

D 🔊 **Listen for gist.** Read the sentences. Then listen again. Circle T for *True* or F for *False*. **CD 2 Track 34**

1. Diego's sister probably knew he was lying.   T   F

2. For most people, it's hard to lie well.   T   F

3. If a person won't make eye contact with you, he's probably lying.   T   F

E  **Listen for details.** Answer the questions with a partner. Use information from the lecture to explain.

1. What white lie did Diego tell his sister? Was his lie believable? Why or why not?

2. Can you tell if someone is lying by looking at their eyes? Why or why not?

Do you think the boy is telling the truth to his father?

3 READING

A  **Make connections.** Look at the photo and describe it to a partner. If you got lost in this place, what would you do?

B **Make predictions.** Read the story through line 17. What do you think will happen next? Discuss your ideas with a partner. Then read the rest of the story.

C **Sequence events.** Put the events in the order that they happened.

_____ A note was placed on the car.

_____ The car stopped working.

_____ Philippe and Sophie had tea and local food.

_____ Philippe and Sophie went for a drive.

_____ A strange man showed up.

_____ The hired driver fixed the car.

_____ The hired driver left.

D **Infer meaning.** Find these words in the reading.

1. Find a word in line 6 that means *sleep lightly*: _____

2. Find a word in line 6 that means *strange*: _____

3. Find a word in line 10 that means *far away*: _____

4. Find a word in line 16 that means *smile*: _____

5. Find a word in line 20 that means *excited; very pleased*: _____

6. Find a word in line 25 that means *friendliness to guests*: _____

E  Answer the questions with a partner.

1. Would you have trusted the stranger?

2. Have you ever helped a stranger? If so, what happened?

THE KINDNESS OF STRANGERS

You're cold and alone. You're afraid. You're lost. You can't speak the local language. You've lost your money and passport. You could experience any of these situations in another country. Who would you turn to[1] for help?

My name is Philippe, and my wife's name is Sophie. We're from France. Recently we were faced
5 with a difficult situation while traveling by car in the Alps with our hired driver. It was going to be a long ride, and we were tired. Just as we began to doze, the engine made an odd, loud noise and then stopped working.

The sun was just setting, and the air was getting cooler. We tried communicating with the driver, but with little success. He acted out the act of going to get help, and then he left.

10 We were in a remote location, with no houses in sight. We started to hear the cries of wild animals. Sophie was scared. We didn't have much food, and it was getting colder and darker. I began to lose confidence. Should we leave the car and start walking? Would our driver ever return? Was he a trustworthy man? We were very worried.

A couple of hours passed. Suddenly, the headlights from another car appeared in the dark. An
15 unfamiliar man got out of the car. He looked unfriendly at first, until his mouth opened with a big, friendly grin. He told us that he would help us. He had such a kind face, and we knew we could count on him. We got into his car.

Before we left, he put a note on the windshield of the car with his phone number on it. Then he drove us to a nearby village, and we met his family. His cousin spoke basic French and offered us
20 tea and local foods. Everything was delicious. Everyone asked us questions and were thrilled to have unexpected guests.

Later that evening, the phone rang. It was our driver. He had kept his word and fixed the car. We prepared to leave and thanked our new friends. I couldn't believe the response from the cousin: "No, we thank *you* for coming into our home."

25 I will never forget the warmth and hospitality we received on that day because we relied on a complete stranger for help.

[1]If you *turn to* someone for help, you ask for the person's help.

4 GRAMMAR

A Turn to page 215. Complete the exercises. Then do **B** and **C** below.

Reported Statements with *say* and *tell*		
Quoted speech	**Reported speech**	
"I **am** an honest person."		he **was** an honest person.
"I **trust** you."		he **trusted** me.
"I **don't believe** you."		he **didn't believe** me.
"I'm **leaving**."		he **was leaving**.
"You **lied** to me."	He **said** (that)	I **had lied** to him.
"I'll **call** you tomorrow."	He **told me** (that)	he **would call** me tomorrow.
"We've never **met**."		we **had** never **met**.
"I **may be** late."		he **might be** late.
"You **must work** harder."		I **had to work** harder.
"You **shouldn't talk** to strangers."		I **shouldn't talk** to strangers.

B 🔗 Work with a partner. Follow the steps below.

1. Read the things Dylan told his friends and family members.

2. Take turns reporting what he said to each person. Use *say* or *tell*.

3. Use one of the expressions (*but in reality, in fact…*) to say what the truth is.

Dylan said to his...	But in reality... / in fact... / actually... / the truth is...
1. girlfriend, "I love you."	he wants to break up.
2. classmate Lena, "I'm single."	he's still dating someone.
3. ex-girlfriend, "I hope we can still be friends."	he can't stand his ex.
4. mom, "I'll be home by midnight."	he came home at 2:00 AM.
5. brother, "I didn't borrow and break your laptop."	he did both things.
6. dad, "I've finished my college applications."	he hasn't even started them.
7. friends, "I'm doing an internship at Toyota."	he's working at McDonald's.
8. classmate Sam, "I can't study with you because I'm sick."	he went to a party.

> Dylan said he loved his girlfriend, but in reality he wants to break up.

> Dylan told his classmate Lena that...

C 🔗 Answer the questions with a partner.

1. Has anyone ever lied to you? What did the person say? What was the truth?

2. Have you ever told someone a white lie? What did you say? What was the truth?

> My friend made some cookies. I said they were good, but actually...

5 WRITING

A 🔄 Read the paragraph and finish the story with a partner.

1. Why did the writer lie? What did she say?

2. Did the other person find out the writer was lying? What happened?

B Think about a time you (or someone you know) lied about something. Answer the questions in **A**. Then use your notes and the example to help you write a paragraph of your own.

C 🔄 Exchange your writing with a partner. Read his or her paragraph.

1. Are there any mistakes? If yes, circle them.

2. Answer the questions in **A** about your partner's writing.

3. Return the paper to your partner. Make corrections to your own paragraph.

CAUGHT IN A LIE

Last year, I lied to a classmate of mine. He invited me to go to the movies, but I didn't want to go. I also didn't want to hurt his feelings, so I said that I couldn't go to the movies. Even though I was fine, I said that I was sick. Later that same day, I went shopping with a friend. While we were shopping, I unexpectedly...

6 COMMUNICATION

A 🔄 Work with a partner. Choose a situation about Dylan from the previous page. Create a role play, using reported speech.

Student A: You find out Dylan lied to you about something. Ask him to explain.

Student B: You're Dylan. Try to explain yourself.

GIRLFRIEND: So, Dylan, I was talking to Lena yesterday.

DYLAN: Yeah? What about?

GIRLFRIEND: She said that she had a party at her house.

DYLAN: Oh, I didn't go.

GIRLFRIEND: Oh really? It's obvious that you're lying, because she said...

B 👥 Perform your role play for another pair. After you listen to the other pair, answer this question: How did Dylan explain his behavior? What did he say?

Divers swim with humpback whales
off the coast of Mexico.

Look at the photo. Answer the questions.

1 What animals are in the photo? What do you know about them?

2 What are the people doing? Why do you think they are doing this?

3 What is one way that humans might be affecting these animals and their natural habitat?

UNIT GOALS

1 Describe rare animals and their habitats

2 Ask questions in an indirect way

3 Offer another opinion

4 Talk about man-made structures and their impact on the environment

Walter Fuller walks down Ormond Beach, California.

1 VIDEO The Steward of Ormond Beach

A Read the title. What is a *steward*? What do you think a steward of a beach does?

B ▶ Watch the video. Circle *True* or *False* for each item.

1. Walter Fuller is the steward for Ormond Beach.	True	False
2. His other title is "protector of sea life of Ormond."	True	False
3. For the past 15 years, Walter has been living at Ormond Beach.	True	False
4. In the beginning, Walter visited the beach on his days off.	True	False
5. There are many wetland areas on the Southern California coast.	True	False
6. Walter used to be a volunteer.	True	False
7. In high school, Walter studied the eagle family.	True	False
8. The coastline is considered to be a beautiful part of the United States.	True	False
9. Walter says that having a job motivates him.	True	False

C 🗘 Answer these questions. Share your answers with a partner.

1. What area do you know that needs a steward? _____

2. Why did you choose that area? _____

2 VOCABULARY

A Work with a partner. You are going to learn about two different animals. Follow the instructions below. Look up any words you don't know.

Student A: Read the information about **snow leopards**.

Student B: Read the information about **mountain gorillas**.

Snow leopards

We don't know exactly how many snow leopards there are, but we do know their numbers are **declining**. Today, there may be as few as 3,000 **in the wild**.

The secretive animals live in the countries of Central Asia, but people **rarely** see them.

They have thick fur that helps them survive the cold winters of their mountain **environment**.

The leopards like to eat sheep and goats, and for this reason, many are killed by sheepherders.

Mountain gorillas

Mountain gorillas live in **dense** forests. They can climb trees, but spend most of their time on the ground.

They are found in Africa—in Rwanda and Congo.

The gorillas are **endangered** (currently only 900 **remain**) due to **illegal** hunting and loss of their **habitat**.

Even so, their numbers are slowly **increasing** because they are **protected**.

B Interview your partner about his or her animal. Ask questions to complete the information in the chart.

	Snow leopard	Mountain gorilla
Population		
Habitat		
Location		
Challenges		

How many snow leopards are there?

C The snow leopard and the mountain gorilla are **suffering**. Both animals are almost **extinct**. What would you do to **raise awareness** of their situations? What would you tell people? Discuss with a partner.

3 LISTENING

A 🔄 **Use background knowledge.** Look at the photo. What animal is this? What do you know about it? Discuss with a partner.

B 🔊 **Listen for details.** Listen to four descriptions of animals that live in the rainforest. Circle the correct words to complete the definitions. **CD 2 Track 36**

Listening 1 *Rodent* means dog / rat.
　　　　　　To exceed means to be greater / lesser than (an amount).

Listening 2 *Snout* means nose / legs.
　　　　　　Nocturnal means active / inactive at night.

Listening 3 *To camouflage* means to escape / to hide.
　　　　　　To inhabit means to eat / to live.

Listening 4 *An acrobat* does tricks on the ground / in the air.
　　　　　　To leap means to jump / to fall.

C 🔊 **Listen for numbers.** Listen again. Complete the sentences with the numbers in the box. Three numbers are extra. **CD 2 Track 36**

1	1.12	1.2	5	12	66	68	135	138	180

Capybara　　　　1. can hold its breath underwater for up to _____ minute(s)

　　　　　　　　2. can weigh up to _____ kilo(s)

　　　　　　　　3. can be more than _____ meter(s) long

Tapir　　　　　　4. weighs between _____ and _____ kilo(s)

Sloth　　　　　　5. comes down to the ground _____ time(s) a week

Spider monkey　　6. can jump over _____ meter(s)

D Look at the photo in **A** again. What animal is it? How do you know?

WORLD LINK

Choose one of the animals. Go online and learn one more fact about it. Share the fact with the class.

4 SPEAKING

A 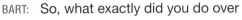 Gustav and Carolina are telling Bart about their summer job. Listen to and read their conversation. Where did they work and what did they do? Why can't Bart apply for the job? **CD 2 Track 37**

BART: So, what exactly did you do over the summer?

GUSTAV: We worked as volunteers at Glacier National Park.

BART: I've never been there. What's it like?

CAROLINA: It's beautiful. There are mountains and lakes... and, of course, glaciers!

BART: How was the job?

GUSTAV: We had to do a lot of physical work. It was kind of hard.

CAROLINA: That's true, but it was exciting, too! We actually saw bears!

BART: Wow! That *does* sound exciting. Maybe I should apply. I'll need a job next summer.

CAROLINA: Sorry, Bart, but you can't apply to that program. It's a special program for international students.

B Practice the conversation in groups of three.

SPEAKING STRATEGY

C Imagine that you and your partner are looking for a place to live together as roommates. Write down some of the important things to consider.

cost, _____

_____

_____

Useful Expressions
Offering another opinion
That's true, but...
Yes, but on the other hand,...
Even so,...
But then again,...

D Read about these two possible places to live. Add three more ideas to each list. With a partner, discuss the positive and negative aspects of each place. Use the Useful Expressions to help you.

City apartment	Suburban home
expensive	big backyard
near public transportation	need a car
small bedrooms	quiet neighborhood
big balcony with a great view	nothing to do on weekends
_____	_____
_____	_____
_____	_____

An apartment in the city would be expensive.

Yes, but on the other hand, living in the city is exciting. There's so much to do!

E With your partner, have a discussion and then choose one of the places to live in **D**. Tell the class which location you chose and why.

5 GRAMMAR

A Turn to page 216. Complete the exercises. Then do **B–D** below.

Embedded Questions	
What is a tapir?	Do you know **what a tapir is**? I'd like to know **what a tapir is**.
Asking for information	**Saying you don't know something**
Can / Could you tell me… Do you know… Do you remember… Do you have any idea…	I don't know / I'd like to know… I'm not sure… I can't remember… I wonder…

B Find and correct the error in each sentence.

1. Could you tell me what is the answer?

2. Can you remember me how to get there?

3. I'm not sure how to do it?

4. What's your opinion? I like to know what you think.

5. I'm not sure where is the exit.

C Turn each question on the left into an embedded question on the right.

1. Where do they live?   I'd like to _____ where _____.

2. What is their habitat?   Can you _____ me _____?

3. What challenges do they face? Do you _____ any _____ what _____?

4. How much does a capybara weigh? I'm not _____ how much _____.

5. How do sloths sleep?   I wonder _____.

6. Where do tapirs spend their time? I don't know _____.

7. Why are monkeys called "acrobats"? Do you know _____?

8. What is the name of that animal? I can't _____ what _____.

D 🔁 Think of an animal. Take turns asking a partner about his or her animal.

> Can you tell me where red pandas live?

> They're from China.

> What is their habitat?

> I'm not sure what their habitat is. Maybe they live in the mountains.

6 COMMUNICATION

A Work alone. Take the quiz. Look up any words you don't know.

A *harbor* is a protected area of water where boats are protected from storms.

What / Where is the world's...

1. busiest harbor?
   a. Singapore
   b. Pusan (South Korea)
   c. Hong Kong (China)

2. largest island?
   a. Great Britain
   b. Greenland (Denmark)
   c. Honshu (Japan)

3. highest waterfall?
   a. Tugela Falls (South Africa)
   b. Angel Falls (Venezuela)
   c. Sutherland Falls (New Zealand)

4. oldest active volcano?
   a. Kilauea (US)
   b. Yasur (Vanuatu)
   c. Etna (Italy)

5. longest mountain range?
   a. the Austrian Alps (Europe)
   b. the Andes (South America)
   c. the Urals (Europe)

6. longest cave?
   a. Mammoth Cave (US)
   b. Holloch Cave (Switzerland)
   c. Sistema Ox Bel Ha (Mexico)

7. deepest lake?
   a. Lake Superior (US / Canada)
   b. Lake Nyasa (Africa)
   c. Lake Baikal (Russia)

8. largest desert?
   a. the Sahara (North Africa)
   b. the Australian (Australia)
   c. the North American (Mexico / US)

9. longest coastline?
   a. Australia
   b. Canada
   c. Chile

B Get into a group of four people. Imagine that you are on a quiz show. Follow the steps below.

> Maria, do you know what the largest island in the world is?

> I'm not sure what the answer is, but I chose Great Britain. Is that correct?

Student A: quiz show announcer

Students B–D: quiz show contestants

1. **Student A:** Read a question from the quiz in **A**.

2. **Students B–D:** Write down your answer on a piece of paper.

3. **Student A:** Ask each contestant for his or her answer. Then check page 218 and give each contestant one point for a correct answer. Continue asking questions.

4. **Students B–D:** The person with the most points at the end of the game wins.

The Burj Khalifa, Dubai, United Arab Emirates

- This skyscraper is the tallest building in the world at 829.8 meters (2,722 feet).

- Architects **proposed** ideas for the building in 2003 and **construction** was finished in 2010.

- Architects faced many **obstacles** in building a skyscraper this big. The building needed to be very strong to **withstand** its own weight! The extreme heat of Dubai also had to be **considered**.

- Another issue was how to safely and quickly **transport** people and **goods** around the building. The builders found an **efficient** solution to **get around** this problem. The building has 57 high-speed elevators. Each can travel 600 meters a minute and **accommodate** 10–12 people.

- The building has many **sustainable** features as well. For example, it collects and reuses water from the air conditioners, saving 15 million gallons of water a year!

1 VOCABULARY

A 🔄 What do you know about the famous building in this photo? Tell a partner. Then take turns reading about it aloud.

B 🔄 Complete the sentences using the words in **blue** from above. Work with a partner.

1. Engineers need to make sure the skyscraper can ____withstand____ earthquakes before they start _____.

2. There are other _____ to think about, too. For example, where will people park?

3. To answer this question, the architect _____ an idea: build an underground parking lot. It will be able to _____ 1,500 cars.

4. From the parking lot, an elevator will _____ people and goods to the top floor in 15 seconds.

5. The team _____ the architect's idea and agreed with his suggestion.

6. There should also be a(n) _____ way of heating and cooling the building.

7. With solar panels, the building will have plenty of energy and also be _____.

C 🔄 Discuss the questions with a partner.

1. Why is the Burj Khalifa special?

2. What were some of the obstacles that architects faced when they designed it?

3. What's special about the building's elevators?

4. How is the building good for the environment?

2 LISTENING

A  Which words in the box do you know? With a partner, look up any unfamiliar words in your dictionary.

architect	edge	investigate
blueprint	get access (to a place)	leaky

B 🔊 **Listen for gist.** Which photo shows what the woman does in her job? Listen and circle the correct one. **CD 2 Track 38**

C 🔊 **Listen for details.** Listen. Complete the sentences about Jamie's job. **CD 2 Track 38**

1. Jamie works with _____ buildings.
2. She checks problems so that they don't _____ mistakes.
3. Rappelling is a way to get access to _____ places.
4. After you hook up to the top of the building, you _____ over the edge.
5. Rappelling is scary, but you can get _____.

D 🔊 **Pronunciation: Negative questions to confirm information.** Complete the negative questions. Then listen and check your answers. **CD 2 Track 39**

1. (be / you / an engineer) _Aren't you an engineer?_   That's correct. I'm a civil engineer.
2. (work / you / on the second floor) _____   No, actually I work on the third floor.
3. (be / the Burj Khalifa / in the UAE) _____   Yes, it is, in Dubai.
4. (be / the Eiffel Tower / built in 1900) _____   No. It was finished in 1889.

E  Practice asking and answering questions 1–4 in **D** with a partner. Pay attention to intonation.

A **Use background knowledge; Make predictions.** Look at the title and the names of the two countries in the article. Do you know anything about these countries? What do you think is happening in these countries?

B **Take notes on key details.** Read the article. As you read, think about questions 1 and 2. Underline the information in the passage that answers the questions.

1. How are rising sea levels affecting the Seychelles and the Netherlands specifically?

2. What is each country doing about these problems?

C **Infer meaning.** Match the words in bold in the reading with their definitions.

_____ a short description

_____ planned pieces of work

_____ to damage land or rock so it disappears

_____ close to the height of the ocean

_____ walls built across bodies of water to hold the water back

D 🔄 **Summarize; Give opinions.** Answer the questions with a partner.

1. Look again at the questions in **B**. Explain your answers to a partner in your own words.

2. Has global warming affected the area where you live? What do you think can be done to help?

WHEN THE SEAS RISE

A solar-powered floating house in Rotterdam, the Netherlands.

When most people think of global warming[1], they think of something that will happen in the future, something that doesn't affect their daily life. But for many people around the world, the future is now. Research shows that sea levels worldwide have been rising at a rate of 0.14 inches (3.5 millimeters) per year since the early 1990s. The trend, linked to global warming, is putting thousands of coastal cities at risk of being destroyed over time. The two countries below offer a **snapshot** of what climate change might look like for all of us.

Seychelles

This chain of islands in the Indian Ocean has been called one of the most beautiful places on Earth. There is a problem, though. Many of the country's most populated regions were constructed in **low-lying** areas, near the water. As sea levels rise, many people will lose their homes.

Already, the island's tourism industry is being hurt. Seychelles's famous beaches are being **eroded** by the rising water, as well as by storms that grow more powerful each year. In addition, the country's coral reefs (a popular tourist attraction) are suffering because of warmer water.

To fight these problems, the government of the Seychelles has been trying to relocate people living in low-lying coastal areas to higher ground. Unfortunately, there isn't enough land to accommodate many of these people. The country's citizens are also trying to bring as much attention as possible to global warming and the danger it poses. They point out that if these things happen to the Seychelles, they can happen to big countries like the United States, China, or Brazil next.

The Netherlands

For the people of the Netherlands, rising waters have been an obstacle for years. The country is close to 30 percent under sea level! A series of **dams and dikes** has protected the country from mass flooding for many years, but as sea levels continue to rise, more extreme solutions are being considered. One of them is a large increase in "floating houses." These houses are built on water or in areas that flood, and each structure is able to rise and fall with the water. Sustainable and efficient apartment buildings that can float are also being planned.

Engineers in the Netherlands are also continuing the country's tradition of doing large construction **projects** to help hold the water back. Larger dams have been built in recent years, and rivers have been rerouted so they are not as close to cities. Today, engineers from many countries visit the Netherlands to learn more about these projects. They fear that in the future, as the Earth warms and sea levels continue to rise, Dutch building techniques will have to be used all over the world.

[1]*Global warming* is an increase in the Earth's temperature, caused in part by humans' use of fossil fuels (oil, gas). As the Earth warms, ice melts, causing sea levels to rise.

4 GRAMMAR

A Turn to page 217. Complete the exercises. Then do **B** below.

The Passive with Various Tenses		
	Active	**Passive**
Simple present	Engineers <u>build</u> skyscrapers with a steel frame structure.	Most skyscrapers **are built** with a steel frame structure.
Simple past	The Woolworth Company <u>built</u> a skyscraper in 1913.	One of the first skyscrapers **was built** in 1913.
Present perfect	Engineers <u>have built</u> the world's tallest building in Dubai.	The world's tallest building **has been built** in Dubai.
Present continuous	Engineers <u>are building</u> a lot of tall buildings in Shanghai.	A lot of tall buildings **are being built** in Shanghai.
Simple future	Someday they <u>will build</u> a skyscraper without concrete.	Someday a skyscraper without concrete **will be built**.

B 👥 Work with a partner. Follow the steps below.

1. Read the information below. Look up the underlined words in a dictionary.

2. Each person should choose a role (Student A or B).

3. Debate the issue with your partner. In your own words, explain what you want to do. Give two reasons to support your opinion. Try to agree about what to do.

4. Share your plan with another pair.

A large construction company wants to <u>tear down</u> traditional buildings in a neighborhood in your city. The buildings are beautiful, but they were built 100 years ago and aren't in good condition.

Student A: You work for the construction company. Here is your plan:

- The old buildings will be torn down, and new office and apartment buildings will be built.

- The new buildings will be safer and will be able to accommodate more people.

- Former <u>tenants</u> will be allowed to move back into a new apartment, but it will take three years for the project to be finished. For now, those people must find other housing.

Student B: You live in one of the old buildings now. You have this opinion:

- A lot of modern buildings have been built in our city. Older structures should be <u>preserved</u>.

- Many people in the buildings are elderly. They shouldn't be <u>forced</u> to leave their homes.

The old buildings should be preserved. They connect us with our past.

Yes, but on the other hand, these old buildings may not withstand...

5 WRITING

A What do you think about the issue in Grammar **B**? In five minutes, outline your ideas below. Then, in 20 minutes, write a paragraph. Explain each reason with an extra sentence or two.

In my opinion, the old buildings should / shouldn't be torn down for two reasons.

For one thing, _____.

In addition, _____.

For these reasons, I believe the old buildings should / shouldn't be torn down.

B 🔁 Exchange your writing with a partner. Circle any mistakes in your partner's writing. Do you agree with your partner's opinion? Why or why not? Return the paper to your partner. Make corrections to your own paragraph.

6 COMMUNICATION

A 🔁 Read about Diamond City's problems. What projects have been proposed to solve these problems? Use your own words to explain each situation with a partner.

Problem 1: The dam was built 30 years ago, and it is weak. **Project:** Repair the dam. This will take three years. **Notes:** The city has been hit by a huge flood every 100 years. The last flood was 20 years ago, and the downtown area was destroyed.	**Problem 3:** The traffic is terrible, and businesses are leaving the city because of it. **Project:** Build a new subway line to transport people. It will take three years to finish. **Notes:** Construction will be difficult and expensive, but a new subway system is needed to transport people.
Problem 2: The baseball stadium is old. **Project:** Repair the stadium. It will take two years. **Notes:** The Diamond City Miners baseball team is a big moneymaker for the city. But if the stadium isn't fixed soon, the team may move to another city.	**Problem 4:** There isn't enough office space in Diamond City. **Project:** Build a new skyscraper to keep businesses in the city. It will take two years to finish. **Notes:** The land around the skyscraper is polluted and must be cleaned up first. This will take a year or more. Then construction can begin.

B 🔁 With your partner, rank the projects in the order you would do them. Give reasons for your order. Note: A new project can be started only after the previous one has been finished.

C 👥 Explain your plan from **B** to another pair. Are your ideas similar? If not, whose plan is better? Why?

1 STORYBOARD

A Lisa is asking Ana about her recent vacation. Look at the pictures and complete the conversation. More than one answer may be possible for each blank.

B ⟳ Practice the conversation with a partner. Then change roles and repeat.

C ⟳ What do you think of Ana's idea? What would you do to raise awareness? Tell a partner.

2 SEE IT AND SAY IT

A Study the picture for ten seconds and then close your book. With a partner, take turns describing the scene in as much detail as you can.

B Look at the picture again. Answer the questions with a partner.

1. Who are these people? Where are they?

2. Where are they going or what are they looking for? What time of day is it?

3. What do you think the leader is thinking?

C What would you do if you were the leader of the group? Make suggestions and explain your answers with a partner.

> It's getting late. They should stop. If I were the leader, I'd suggest we sleep in the cave.

> That's one idea. But then again, I think the cave would be too cold. I'd suggest...

3 SARA AND SANDRA

A Read the story about Sara and Sandra. Fill in the missing words.

Sara and Sandra are sisters. They both _____ it rich by

_____ the lottery.

Sara decided she could _____ by on very little money. She made a very

tight budget for herself. She took 50 percent of the money and _____

it to charities. She also _____ aside the _____ amount in

a bank _____.

Sandra, on the other hand, did something different. She _____

her money on jewelry, vacations, and presents for herself. She spent way

_____ much money and didn't _____ anything. In one

year, she had _____ into debt and _____ afford to pay

_____ all the money she had borrowed.

B With a partner, compare your answers in **A**.

C Imagine your friend has won the lottery. Give him or her some financial advice. Use the negative modals in the box.

don't have to	had better not	shouldn't

> Well, for one thing, you don't have to tell everyone right away.

4 LISTENING

A Listen to each response. Then choose the question that came before the response. **CD 2 Track 41**

1. a. ☐ What does she look like?
   b. ☐ What's she like?

2. a. ☐ Why did you buy a new car?
   b. ☐ Why do you want a new car?

3. a. ☐ What would you do if you won the contest?
   b. ☐ What will you do when you win the contest?

4. a. ☐ Did you like the painting?
   b. ☐ How long did it take you to paint it?

5. a. ☐ When did they complete the bridge?
   b. ☐ When will they complete the bridge?

6. a. ☐ What do you usually do on Friday night?
   b. ☐ What do you want to do on Friday night?

5 WHILE YOU WERE OUT

A  Imagine that, while your boss was out, you took several messages. Work with a partner. Using reported speech, give the messages to your boss. Then switch roles and repeat.

> **Student A:** Give these messages to your boss.
>
> 1. Mary: "The meeting is scheduled for 2:00."
>
> 2. Tom: "I won't be in the office next week. I'll be in China on business."
>
> 3. Copy company: "We're running behind schedule on your job."
>
> **Student B:** Give these messages to your boss.
>
> 1. Celine: "I can't make the deadline."
>
> 2. Dry cleaners: "Your suits are ready."
>
> 3. Mario: "I don't understand your memo. I have questions about it."

> Were there any messages while I was out?

> Yes. There were three. Mary called. She said that...

6 MAKING PLANS

A With a partner, choose a situation and create a conversation of eight to ten sentences.

Situation 1	Situation 2
Student A: There's a Broadway show in town, and your partner wants to see it. You think the show is too expensive.	**Student A:** There's a popular art exhibit at the museum. Your partner wants to see it. You think it will be very crowded and hard to see the paintings.
Student B: There's a Broadway show in town, and you really want to see it. Persuade your partner to go.	**Student B:** There's an exhibition at the museum in town, and you really want to see it. Persuade your partner to go.

B: I really want to see the Broadway show that's in town.

A: Yes, but it's too expensive.

B: That's true, but...

B Practice your conversation. Then perform it for another pair.

UNIT **1** INDOORS AND OUTDOORS

LESSON A

Vocabulary

color
bright ~, dark ~, favorite ~,
  neutral ~, primary ~

combine
get rid of
home improvement
option
overwhelming

rearrange
rebuild
recreate
redo
repaint
repair
replace
restart
work well

Speaking Strategy

Making informal suggestions
With base form
Why don't you <u>fix</u> it yourself?
I think you should <u>fix</u> it yourself.
I know what you should do. <u>Call</u>
  my friend.

With verb + -ing
Have you thought about <u>fixing</u>
  it yourself?
Try <u>calling</u> my friend.

Responding
Strong yes
Good idea!
That's a great idea.
Sounds good to me.

Weak yes
I guess it's worth a try.
Maybe I'll do that.

No
I don't think so.
No, I don't like that idea.

LESSON B

Vocabulary

disturb
litter
no one else's business
preserve

privacy
have (no) privacy

public
the general public
open to the public

public / private
~ conversation, ~ figure,
  ~ life, ~ school, ~ space, in ~

publicly / privately
~ owned business

rights

UNIT 2 MILESTONES

LESSON A

Vocabulary

infant (baby) / infancy
toddler
child (kid) / childhood
adolescent (teenager) /
  adolescence
young adult
adult (grown-up) / adulthood

start a family

Speaking Strategy

Talking about plans
planning + infinitive
  I'm planning to take a driving test.
going to + base form
  I'm going to visit my cousins.
thinking about + gerund
  I'm thinking about taking a trip.

Talking about needs
need + infinitive
  I need (to rent) a car.

LESSON B

Vocabulary

be born
buy a house
enroll (in college)
fall in love
get a job
get divorced
get married
get pregnant
go to school
have children
leave home
raise a family
retire

UNIT 3 GETTING INFORMATION

LESSON A

Vocabulary

argue / argument
    get into an argument
converse / conversation
    strike up / start a
        conversation
    carry on a conversation
chat / chat
    chat with your coworkers
discuss / discussion
    a discussion of (the plan)
gossip / gossip
    the latest gossip
    a piece of gossip
    juicy gossip
share
    share your (feelings / ideas)
talk / talk
    give a talk, listen to a talk

argue / converse / chat / gossip /
  share / talk (*with* someone,
  about something)
discuss (something *with*
  someone)
have a(n) argument / conversation /
  chat / discussion / talk

Speaking Strategy

Interrupting someone politely
Introducing yourself
Excuse me. May I interrupt for
  a moment? My name is…
I'm sorry to interrupt. / I beg your
  pardon.
I just wanted to introduce myself.
  My name is…

Interrupting someone you know
Excuse me. Sorry to bother you,
  (name), but I have a question.
Could I interrupt for a second?
  I just wanted to say / ask
  something.

LESSON B

Vocabulary

media
in the media

news
get (your) news
in the news
tell (someone) the news
(news) source
news **story**
(**local / national / international**)
  news
(**entertainment / sports /
  tabloid**) news
(news) **program / site**
**bad, good, great, sad,
  sensational** (news)
spread the, hear the news

accurate ↔ inaccurate
reliable ↔ unreliable
scandal

word of mouth

UNIT **4** MEN AND WOMEN

LESSON A

Vocabulary

brush your (hair / teeth)
color / **dye** your hair
get a (haircut / manicure / tattoo)
get your ears pierced
have (your nails done / your hair curled / your teeth straightened)
neaten up
shave your (face / head / legs)
straighten your hair
stand out
strike a pose
wear (cologne / perfume / deodorant / makeup / bright colors)

Speaking Strategy

Disagreeing politely
I agree up to a point.
Yes, but… / I know, but…
I'm not sure. / I don't know.
But what about (the cost)?
I'm not sure it's / that's (such) a good idea. Are you sure?
I see what you're saying / you mean, but…
I see where you're coming from, but…

LESSON B

Vocabulary

Separable phrasal verbs
ask (someone) **out**
give (something) up
turn (someone) **down**
turn (something) **on**

Inseparable phrasal verbs
break up (with someone)
cheat on (someone)
get along (with someone)
get over (someone)
go out (with someone)
grow up
make up (with someone)
run into (someone)

UNIT **5** ACROSS CULTURES

LESSON A

Vocabulary

appropriate ↔ **inappropriate**
considerate ↔ **inconsiderate**
crucial
customary
honest ↔ **dishonest**
kind ↔ **unkind**
mature ↔ **immature**
normal
polite ↔ **impolite, rude**
pleasant ↔ **unpleasant**
respectful ↔ **disrespectful**
responsible ↔ **irresponsible**
sincere ↔ **insincere**

Speaking Strategy

Asking about culturally appropriate behavior
Is it OK / appropriate to use my fingers?
Is it OK if I use my fingers?
  Please, go right ahead.
  Absolutely.
  Actually, it's probably better to use a fork.
  Normally, people use a fork.
Is it all right to wear shoes inside?
Is it all right if I wear shoes inside?
  Sure, no problem.
  Yeah, it's fine.
  Actually, it's best to remove your shoes.
  No, you really should take off your shoes.

LESSON B

Vocabulary

body language
discouraged
eating habits
(make) **eye contact**
facial expression
homesick
(have, avoid) **jet lag**
(overcome a) **language barrier**
personal space
(make) **small talk**

LESSON A

Vocabulary

advertise → **advertisement** →
  advertiser
consume → **consumption** →
  consumer
develop → **development** →
  developer
employ → **employment** →
  employer
invest → **investment** → **investor**
manage → **management** →
  manager
produce → **production** →
  producer
promote → **promotion** →
  promoter
purchase
ship → **shipment** → **shipper**

Speaking Strategy

Asking about companies
What does your company
  do exactly?
What is the main focus of your
  company?
How do you... ?

Emphasizing important points
I'd like to emphasize that...
Never forget that...
This is a key point.
The bottom line is...

LESSON B

Vocabulary

catchy
clever
a **dramatic increase** / **increase**
  dramatically
get better ↔ get worse
increase ↔ decrease
inspiring
persuasive
profits
recover
a **sharp fall** / **fall sharply**
shocking
a **slight rise** / **rise slightly**
(in a) **slump**
a **steady decline** / **decline**
  steadily
(be) up ↔ (be) down

UNIT 7 WELLBEING

LESSON A

Vocabulary

can't stop + *-ing* verb: I can't stop
(**coughing** / scratching /
shivering / sneezing).
feel + adjective: I feel (**dizzy** /
nauseous / **drowsy** / **exhausted** /
faint / **weak** / sick).
have + noun: I have (a
stomachache / an earache /
a backache / a toothache / a
cut / a sore throat / a fever / a
temperature / a cold / the flu).
possessive adjective + noun +
hurt: My (arm / finger / back /
stomach) hurts. / My legs hurt.
blink
breathe
chew
make sense
swallow symptom

Speaking Strategy

Giving serious advice
In my opinion, you should…
I always advise people to…
I think the best idea (for you)
  is to…
If I were you, I'd…

Accepting advice
You're right. Thanks for the advice.
That makes (a lot of) sense. I'll
  give it a try.
I'll try it and get back to you.

Refusing advice
I'm not sure that would work for me.
That doesn't (really) make sense
  to me.
I could never do that.

LESSON B

Vocabulary

care: take ~ of, ~ about

sick: make someone ~,
  call in ~, ~ day,
  ~ of (something /
  someone), **worried ~**
homesick, carsick, lovesick,
  seasick

well: do ~, ~ behaved, ~ **paid,**
  might (may) **as ~**

boss around
chaos
cut class
fatigue
gentle
ground (= punish) someone
massage
meditation
paralyze
straightforward
tidy
treat (someone) like (a kid)
yoga

UNIT 8 THE ACTIVE LIFE

LESSON A

Vocabulary

activity:
be into / be involved in /
  participate in / take part in an ~
spare / leisure time ~
physical, mental, outdoor,
  extracurricular, classroom ~

active:
stay / remain ~
highly / extremely / very ~
fairly, increasingly ~
mentally, **physically** ~

athlete:
amateur, professional, serious ~

Speaking Strategy

**Explaining the set-up and rules
of a game**
It's played with…
You don't need any special
  equipment.
There are 11 players on each
  team. / You compete against
  each other.
One team starts by… / The game
  begins when…
The team with the most points
  wins. / The object is to score the
  most runs.
It's played on a field. / It's played
  all over the world.

LESSON B

Vocabulary

ask for
believe in
dominate
go to your head
head out
learn about
pay for
prepare for
spend on
stay in
warn about

UNIT 9 SOCIAL ISSUES

LESSON A

Vocabulary

as usual
campaign
candidate
citizen
clear (adj)
corporation
enthusiastically
expand
give it your best shot
launch (v)
make progress
never in my wildest dreams
raise taxes
(a) record turnout
reelect
running neck and neck
tax (v)
term
up for reelection
vote (for ↔ against)
voting age
vow (v)

Speaking Strategy

Language for presentations

Stating the purpose
Today, I'd like to talk to you
 about…
I'll begin by (talking about the
 issue). / I'll provide an overview
 of (the issue).
Then I'll list the (two / three /
 four)…

Stating important points
Let's talk first about… / Let's start
 by talking about…
One of the main causes of (traffic)
 is…
Another / A second cause
 of (traffic) is…
And finally…

LESSON B

Vocabulary

a change of scene
depression
destroy → **destruction**
develop → **development**
disabled
encourage → **encouragement**
force → **force**
improve → **improvement**
protect → **protection**
provide
put down roots
rely (on) → **reliance**
sprawl
spread
suburban
support → **support**
urban
wait and see
waste → **waste**

UNIT 10 MONEY

LESSON A

Vocabulary

afford
broke
(make a / have a) budget
borrow ↔ **lend** (**money**)
get by
go into debt
owe
pay back
save ↔ **spend** (money)
short on cash
stick to it

Speaking Strategy

Apologizing
Small accident or mistake
I'm sorry. It was an accident.
Sorry. My mistake.
I can't believe I did that.

Serious accident or mistake
I'm really sorry that I forgot to…
I'm so sorry about damaging…
I want to apologize for what
 happened.

Accepting an apology
Don't worry about it.
Oh, that's OK.
No problem. It happens.
Apology accepted.

LESSON B

Vocabulary

affordable
donate (money)
earn / **make** (money)
earnings
invest (money)
millionaire
set aside / **save** ↔ **spend**
 (money)
squander / **waste** (money)
strike it rich
valuable
wealthy

UNIT 11 HONESTY

LESSON A

Vocabulary

against the law
an honest person ↔ a liar
(**depend on the**) **circumstances**
exception
hurt (**someone's feelings**)
obvious
reward someone ↔ punish
someone (**for their behavior**)
tell the truth ↔ tell a lie

Speaking Strategy

Giving strong advice
If you don't leave a bigger tip,
the waiter is going to be upset.
I don't think you should spend
so much time playing games
on your computer.
You have to do your homework
by yourself.

LESSON B

Vocabulary

actually
catch someone
counting on
but in fact
have confidence in
in reality
keep my word
make excuses
trick people
the truth is
trust
trustworthy
truthful
turn to
white lie

UNIT 12 OUR WORLD

LESSON A

Vocabulary

dense
endangered
environment
extinct
habitat
illegal
increase ↔ decline
protected
raise awareness
rare / **rarely**
remain
suffer
(in the) **wild**
wilderness

Speaking Strategy

Offering another opinion
That's true, but…
Yes, but on the other hand,…
Even so,…
But then again,…

LESSON B

Vocabulary

accommodate
considered
construction
dam
dike
efficient
erode
force (someone to do something)
get around
goods
low-lying
obstacle
project
proposed
snapshot
sustainable
tear down (a building)
tenant
transport
withstand

UNIT 1 INDOORS AND OUTDOORS

LESSON A

Active Voice			Stative Passive Voice		
Subject	**Verb**	**Object**	**Subject**	***be***	**Past participle**
❶ I	broke	the window.	❷ The window	is	broken.

Sentence ❶ describes an action or event: *I broke the window.*

Sentence ❷ is in the stative passive. It describes a state of being. There is no action taking place: *The window is broken (because I broke it).*

The object in an active sentence becomes the subject in a passive sentence.

The past participle is a verb form that functions as an adjective after the verb *be*.

Base, Simple Past, and Past Participle Forms								
Base	**Simple past**	**Past participle**	**Base**	**Simple past**	**Past participle**	**Base**	**Simple past**	**Past participle**
bend	bent	bent	close	closed	closed	jam	jammed	jammed
break	broke	broken	crack	cracked	cracked	pack	packed	packed
burn	burned	burned	flood	flooded	flooded	ruin	ruined	ruined
clog	clogged	clogged	freeze	froze	frozen	stain	stained	stained

Verbs that are regular in the simple past take the same *-ed* ending for the past participle: *burn / burned / burned*.

Verbs that are irregular in the simple past have irregular past participle forms: *freeze / froze / frozen*.

A Use the correct verb + *be* to describe each picture below.

1. The mirror
   is cracked .

2. The light bulbs
   _____.

3. The basement
   _____.

4. The lock
   _____.

5. The drain
   _____.

6. The keys
   _____.

B Use the words in parentheses to make an active sentence in the simple past. Then rewrite it in the stative passive voice.

1. (I / crack / the mirror)   a. *I cracked the mirror.*   b. *The mirror is cracked.*

2. (she / break / the lock)   a. _____   b. _____

3. (they / pack / their suitcases)   a. _____   b. _____

4. (he / close / the door)   a. _____   b. _____

5. (cold weather / freeze / the pipes) a. _____   b. _____

C Complete the sentences with the correct form of the words in parentheses.

1. This room needs a lot of work. The walls (crack) _____, and the floor (stain) _____.

2. It rained a lot, and now the house (flood) _____.

3. Don't (jam) _____ the key into the lock. You don't want to (break) _____ it.

4. Someone (break) _____ the window last week, and it _____ still (break) _____.

5. The little boy (throw) _____ something into the sink. Now the drain (clog) _____.

6. What's the best thing to do when your car door (freeze) _____?

7. This key doesn't work because it (bend) _____.

LESSON B

Giving Permission and Expressing Prohibition				
	be	**allowed / permitted / supposed to**	**Base form**	
You	**are**	allowed to / permitted to	park	here.
	aren't	supposed to		
	Modal		**Base form**	
You	**can**		park	here.
	can't			
	must			
	must not			

Use *(not) be allowed / permitted to* or *can / can't* to give or deny permission to do something.

Use *be supposed to* to say that someone is expected to do something.

(Not) be supposed to means that you are not allowed to do something.

Use *must / must not* for formal rules and warnings. It is more common to use *can / can't* for prohibition in normal spoken English.

No	**Gerund**	**be**	**allowed / permitted**	
	Talking	**is**(n't)	allowed / permitted	during the test.
No	**talking**			

You can use a gerund + *(not) be allowed / permitted* to give or deny permission.

No + gerund is often used on signs to say something is not allowed.

A Unscramble the words to make sentences.

1. allowed to / He / an hour of TV a week / watch / is

   _____.

2. isn't / in class / Eating / permitted

   _____.

3. permitted to / stay out / She's / until midnight with her friends

   _____.

4. here / is not / Parking / allowed

   _____.

5. supposed to / to school / aren't / wear shorts / We

   _____.

B Circle any mistakes in the dialogs and correct them.

1. A: Excuse me, sir? Sorry, but no parking here today.

   B: Really? I'm always allowed park here on Saturdays.

   A: I know, but they're filming a commercial today. Try garage B. Parking is by permit there.

2. A: What time does school start?

   B: We're suppose be at school by 8:45, but class doesn't start until 9:00.

3. A: During the test, talk is not allowed.

   B: Are we allowed to using a calculator?

   A: Yes, using a calculator is allow.

C Are the things in **A** true for you? Write your answers.

1. <u>I'm allowed to watch more than an hour of TV a week.</u>   .

2. _____ .

3. _____ .

4. _____ .

5. _____ .

UNIT **2** MILESTONES

LESSON A

Review of Future Forms		
Predictions with *be going to* and *will*	Your children **will go to** a good school. Your children **are going to go to** a good school. Do you think your children **will go to** / **are going to go to** a good school? She's **going to have** a baby. ~~She'll have a baby.~~	Use either *will* or *be going to* for general predictions about the future. When the prediction is immediate and based on evidence you can see, use *be going to* (but not *will*).
Quick decisions with *will*	A: Oh, no. The baby is crying! B: Don't worry. **I'll help**.	Use only *will* for quick decisions or offers made at the time of speaking.
Future plans with *be going to* and the present continuous	The teenagers **are going to work** part-time jobs this summer. The teenagers **are working** part-time jobs this summer.* Someday **I'm going to write** a book about my childhood. ~~Someday I'm writing a book about my childhood.~~	Use either *be going to* or the present continuous to talk about future plans. When the future plan is indefinite, use *be going to* (but not the present continuous).
Scheduled events with three future forms	The kids **are going** to summer camp on August 2. The kids **are going to go** to summer camp on August 2. The kids **go** to summer camp on August 2. The kids' summer camp **starts** on August 2 and **ends** on August 10.	You can use *be going to*, the present continuous, or the simple present for scheduled events. The simple present is usually used for events that happen regularly and cannot easily be changed.

*You often need a time expression (like *this summer*) to make the future meaning clear.

A Circle the best answer. In some cases, both answers are correct.

Conversation 1

A: I'll fly / I'm flying to Thailand tomorrow. My plane leaves / is leaving at 4:00.

B: Which suitcase do you take / are you taking?

A: Let's see... I think I'll take / I'm going to take the brown one.

B: You're so lucky. Someday I'm going to visit / I'm visiting Thailand, too!

Conversation 2

A: When is the game?

B: Kickoff is / is being at 7 PM.

A: Our team will definitely win / is definitely going to win tonight.

B: I think so, too. But they may cancel the game.

A: Why?

B: Look at those dark clouds. It will rain / It's going to rain.

LESSON B

Modals of Future Possibility			
Subject	**Modal**	**Main verb**	
I / He / We / They	**may / might / could**	go	to college in the fall.
	may / might not		

You can use *may*, *might*, and *could* to say something is possible (but not certain) in the future.
Note: It's more common to use *may* or *might* than *could* in most affirmative statements.

You can use *may* or *might* with *not*: He **might** / **may not** go to college in the fall.
Don't use *not* with *could* to talk about possibility: ~~He could not go to college in the fall.~~

Yes / No questions and short answers			
With *be*	Will you <u>be</u> home by midnight?	I **may** / **might** / **could** be. I **may** / **might** not be.	I don't know. I'm not sure / certain.
With other verbs	Are you going to <u>go</u> to college?	I **may** / **might** / **could**. I **may** / **might** not.	It's hard to say. We'll see.

You can use *may*, *might*, or *could* to answer questions about the future.

In spoken English, it's common to reply to *Yes / No* questions with a short answer.

It's also common to use expressions like *I don't know.* or *We'll see* in a reply and to give a little more information:

A: *Are you going to go to college?*
B: *I might. I may work for a year first. We'll see.*

A Complete the dialogs with a modal or modal phrase from the chart.

1. A: Are Tim and Jill going to get married?

   B: They _____. They've been dating a long time.

2. A: What are you going to do after college?

   B: I _____ get a job, or I _____ go to graduate school. I'm not sure yet.

3. A: Are you going to study at this school next term?

   B: I _____ . I'm thinking about going to another school.

4. A: Is it going to be cold tonight?

   B: I don't know; it _____ . Take a jacket to be safe.

5. A: Are you going to hang out with your friends this weekend?

   B: I _____ , or I _____ stay home and study.

B Cover the answers in **A**. Answer the questions about yourself. Use modals of future possibility.

1. _____

2. _____

3. _____

4. _____

5. _____

UNIT **3** GETTING INFORMATION

LESSON A

Participial and Prepositional Phrases		
Who is Joe Ortega?	He's the guy	**chatting on the phone.** **on the phone.**
Who is Ms. Anh?	She's the woman	**wearing glasses.** **in front of the class.**
Which books are mine?	They're the ones	**lying on the floor.** **in the drawer.**

Use participial and prepositional phrases to identify people and things. These statements answer questions that ask *who*, *what*, and *which one(s)*.

A present participle uses the form verb + *-ing*. It follows the noun it is modifying: *She's the lady talking to the police officer*.

A prepositional phrase starts with *in*, *on*, *by*, etc. It also follows the noun it is modifying: *He's the man with the mustache*.

A Look at the picture below. What are the people doing? Give each person a name and write a sentence about him or her. Then label the picture.

Who is _____?

He's the man _____ .

_____

_____

_____

_____

_____

_____

B Write questions about the people in the picture. (Use the words in parentheses.)
Start your questions with *Do you know...?*

1. (talk / bus driver) _____ *Do you know the woman talking to the bus driver?* _____

2. (listen / music) _____

3. (skateboard and backpack) _____

4. (school uniforms) _____

5. (talk / phone) _____

6. (suit / briefcase) _____

C 🔗 One a piece of paper, make up your own stories about each person. Use participial and prepositional phrases.

LESSON B

Review of the Present Perfect				
Subject	***have / has*** *(not)*	**Past participle**		
❶ I	**have**(n't)	seen	that news program.	
❶ He	**has**(n't)			
❷ I	**have**(n't)	worked	as a news reporter	**for** six months.
❷ She	**has**(n't)			**since** May.

❶ You can use the present perfect to talk about past actions or experiences when the time they happened is unknown or unimportant.

I have seen that news program.

I haven't been to France.

❷ Use can also use the present perfect to talk about an action that started in the past and continues up to now. Use *for* + a length of time. Use *since* + a point in time.

I have worked as a reporter for six months.

I've lived in Paris since May.

Notice the difference:

present perfect: I've worked as a news reporter for six months. I love my job. (action continues)

simple past: I worked as a news reporter for six months after college. (action is finished)

Questions and short answers					
Wh- word	***have / has***	**Subject**	**Past participle**		**Answers**
	Have	you	heard	the news?	**Yes, I have.** I heard it this morning.* **No, I haven't.** What happened?
How long	**have**	you	been	a reporter?	(I**'ve been** a reporter) **for** six months.
	has	she			(She**'s been** a reporter) **since** May.

* When you answer a present perfect question with a specific time expression, use the simple past:

Have you heard the news? Yes, I heard it this morning.

A 🔁 Complete the conversation. Use the present perfect form of the verb in parentheses, a short answer, or *for* or *since*.

A: (1. hear) __Have__ you _____ the latest news about Leo?

B: No, I (2.) _____. What's up?

A: He's going to be on that reality show *Pop Idol*.

B: Really? How long (3. be) _____ Leo _____ a singer?

A: (4.) _____ high school.

B: I had no idea. (5. see) _____ you ever _____ him perform?

A: Yeah, I (6.) _____. I saw him at a talent show in high school. He was amazing.

UNIT **4** MEN AND WOMEN

LESSON A

Adverbs Used with the Present Perfect			
	With questions	**With affirmative verbs**	**With negative verbs**
ever	Have you **ever** worn makeup?		I haven't **ever** worn makeup.
never		I've **never** worn makeup (before).	
yet	Have you taken a shower **yet**?		I haven't taken a shower **yet**.
still			I **still** haven't taken a shower.
already	Have you **already** taken a shower? Have you taken a shower **already**?	I've **already** taken a shower. I've taken a shower **already**.	
just		I've **just** finished shaving.	

Ever means "at any time." Note: *I haven't ever = I've never*

Never means "not at any time." It is used with an affirmative verb and makes the meaning of the sentence negative. You can add the word *before* for emphasis.

Yet means "up to or until the present time" or "thus far."

Still has a similar meaning to *yet*. It is used for situations that have continued for longer than expected.

Already means something happened and no longer needs to be done. Notice the different placement of *already* in sentences.

Just means "very recently."

A Victor is traveling in Vietnam. Read his email back home. Correct the six errors.

Greetings from Ho Chi Minh City, Vietnam!

There is a lot to see and do here. We've been already here for two days, but there is so much we yet haven't seen. For example, I've already been to the Ben Thanh Market, but I haven't still visited the famous Jade Emperor Pagoda.

By the way, I've come just back from my first ride on a scooter. It was really fun. I haven't never seen so many scooters on the street before!

When are you going to join us? Have already you packed? I can't wait to see you and explore Vietnam with you!

B Circle the sentence that best follows the first sentence.

1. He's never worn bright colors.
   a. He's adventurous.
   b. He's not a risk-taker.

2. I've just met Paula.
   a. She's nice.
   b. She's an old friend.

3. I've already gotten a tattoo.
   a. Should I do it?
   b. I really like it!

4. I haven't washed my hair yet.
   a. I'd better hurry.
   b. It looks much better.

5. I haven't brushed my teeth yet.
   a. I can't find my toothbrush.
   b. My teeth feel so clean!

6. I haven't seen the doctor yet.
   a. I saw him yesterday.
   b. I hope he comes soon.

LESSON B

Phrasal Verbs	
Please **turn on** the TV. Erin **ran into** Alex yesterday.	English has many two-word (phrasal) verbs. These verbs have a verb (like *turn* or *run*) and a smaller word (like *at, along, back, down, in, on, out, over, up, with*).
Please **turn on** <u>the TV</u>. Please **turn** <u>the TV</u> / <u>it</u> **on**. ~~Please **turn on** it.~~	Some phrasal verbs are separable. This means <u>the object</u> (a noun or pronoun) can separate the phrasal verb. **Note:** With separable phrasal verbs, the pronoun *cannot* follow the phrasal verb.
Erin **ran into** <u>Alex</u> / <u>him</u> yesterday.	Many phrasal verbs are inseparable. This means <u>the object</u> (a noun or pronoun) can *only* follow the phrasal verb.
She **grew up** in Mexico City.	Some phrasal verbs do not take an object.
Do you **get along** with Max? Did Sean **ask** her **out**? When did they **break up**? Have you ever **gone out** with him?	Form questions with phrasal verbs the same way you do with other verbs.

Separable phrasal verbs	Inseparable phrasal verbs	
ask (someone) out give (something) up = "stop doing something" turn (someone) down turn (something) on / off	break up (with someone) cheat on (someone) get along (with someone) get over (someone) go out (with someone)	grow up make up (with someone) = "forgive someone and become friends again" run into (someone)

A Unscramble the questions.

1. up / where / you / did / grow

   _____?

2. you / get / do / along / with your family

   _____?

3. out / you / how often / do / with friends / go

   _____?

4. asked / have you ever / out / someone / on a date

   _____?

5. The music is loud. it / you / can / off / turn

   _____?

6. on the way / you / who / into / did / run / to class

   _____?

B Now answer the questions in **A** in complete sentences. Use the phrasal verbs.

1. _____.
2. _____.
3. _____.
4. _____.
5. _____.
6. _____.

UNIT **5** ACROSS CULTURES

LESSON A

		It + be + Adjective + Infinitive ; Gerund + be + Adjective				
It	***be***	**Adjective**	***(for)***	**(pronoun)**	**Infinitive**	
It	**was**(n't)	hard	(for)	(me)	to pass	the test.
It's not		normal	(for)	(us)	to eat	with chopsticks.
It isn't		normal	(for)	(us)	to eat	with chopsticks.
Gerund			***be***	**Adjective**	***(for)***	**(pronoun)**
Passing	the test		**was**(n't)	hard	(for)	(me).
Eating	with chopsticks	**is**(n't)		normal	(for)	(us).

It + be + adjective + infinitive and gerund + *be* + adjective are two different ways of expressing the same thing.

Some adjectives that are commonly used in these patterns are *easy*, *difficult / hard*, *important*, *impossible*, *necessary*, and *wrong*.

For + pronoun is optional because the pronoun is often understood.

You can also use other linking verbs in the place of *be*: *It seems impossible for us to win the game./ At this point, winning the game seems impossible.*

A Read the information about cultural rules in Norway. For each underlined sentence, rewrite it on page 202.

1. People greet each other by shaking hands. At business meetings, it's customary to shake hands when you arrive and when you leave.

2. Business meetings start right on time. Being late is inappropriate.

3. Close friends and family members may hug each other. Hugging people you've just met isn't typical.

4. When you visit someone's home, it's considerate to bring a small gift.

5. Norwegians don't like to waste food. It's polite to finish everything on your plate.

6. Norwegians don't like to say bad things about each other. Being kind to others is very important for them.

7. If you mention "getting together later" to a Norwegian, not following up with a sincere invitation is rude.

8. Norwegians are proud of their distinctive culture. It's disrespectful to treat Norway and Sweden as the same culture.

1. *Shaking hands when you arrive and when you leave is customary.*
2. _____
3. _____
4. _____
5. _____
6. _____
7. _____
8. _____

B 🔄 Now rewrite the sentences in **A** to make similar cultural rules about your country.

Examples:

Bowing when you meet someone is customary.

It's inappropriate to talk to a professor using casual speech.

_____

_____

_____

_____

LESSON B

Present and Future Time Clauses with *before, after, when, as soon as / once*	
Main clause	**Time clause**
❶ In Spain, people often kiss each other	**when** they <u>meet</u>.
❷ Please remove your shoes	**before** you <u>enter</u> the temple.
❸ We're going to go to the park	**after** we <u>eat</u> lunch.
❹ I'll call you	**as soon as** / **once** we <u>arrive</u>.
Time clause	**Main clause**
Before you enter the temple,	please remove your shoes.*

A time clause shows the order of two or more events:

In sentence ❶: *When* shows that two events happen at almost the same time: At the time you meet someone, you kiss them.

In sentence ❷: You remove your shoes first, and then you enter the temple.

In sentence ❸: We plan to eat lunch first, and then we're going to go to the park.

In sentence ❹: *As soon as / Once* means "right after." We arrive, and then I will call you.

When we use time clauses to talk about facts or other information in **the present** (as in ❶ and ❷), the <u>verbs</u> in the main and time clauses are in the present tense. ❷ uses the imperative form with time clauses.

When we use time clauses to talk about **the future** (as in ❸ and ❹):

the <u>verb</u> in the main clause uses a future form.

the <u>verb</u> in the time clause is in the simple present.

*In <u>writing</u>, when the time clause comes first, put a comma before the main clause.

A Alejandro is starting college in Los Angeles soon. Look at his timeline. Then use the words in parentheses to connect the phrases and make sentences about the future.

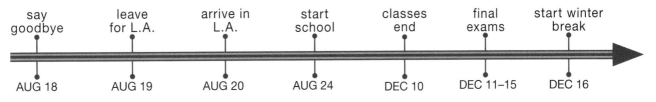

say goodbye	leave for L.A.	arrive in L.A.	start school	classes end	final exams	start winter break
AUG 18	AUG 19	AUG 20	AUG 24	DEC 10	DEC 11–15	DEC 16

1. leave for L.A. / say goodbye to his friends (before)

   _____

2. arrive in L.A. / start school (four days after)

   _____

3. take his final exams / his classes end (once)

   _____

4. start winter break / finish his last exam (as soon as)

   _____

B Complete the sentences below about yourself. Pay attention to the verb forms you use.

1. Before I go home today, _____ .

2. After I eat breakfast in the morning, I

   _____ .

3. I _____ when _____ .

4. I'm going to _____ as soon as _____ .

5. I will _____ once _____ .

BUSINESS AND MARKETING

LESSON A

The Passive Voice: Simple Present and Simple Past			
Subject	**Verb**	**Object**	**Active voice**
Sound Smart	makes	audiobooks.	In an active sentence, the subject is the *agent* (the one performing the action).

Subject	*be*	**Past participle**	**(*by* + Object)**	**Passive voice**
❶ Audiobooks	are	made	by Sound Smart.	In a passive sentence, the object becomes the subject, and the subject becomes the object. The subject is not the agent because it doesn't perform an action.
❷ The products	were	shipped.		
❸ The company	was	founded	by Beverly Smith.	

(Continued)

❶ In a passive sentence, the focus is on the action that happens to the subject, not on who / what performed the action (the agent).

Use *by* + object to indicate the agent: *The Fallingwater house **was built** <u>by Frank Lloyd Wright</u>.*

❷ We don't use *by* + object when the agent is understood, unknown, or unimportant, or when an action is done by people in general.

*I'm **paid** twice a month.* (I know who pays my salary. The agent is understood.)

*All of the money **was stolen**.* (We don't know who did it. The agent is unknown.)

*Once a week, her house **is cleaned**.* (We don't care who does it. The agent is unimportant.)

*Portuguese **is spoken** in Brazil.* (Everyone speaks it. It's done by people in general.)

❸ We include *by* + object in sentences where it sounds incomplete without it.

The company was founded. (By whom? When? This sentence sounds incomplete.)

We can also add a time or place phrase. *The company was founded (by Pablo Ruiz) (in Seattle) (in 2004).*

The form of *be* depends on the verb tense. For the simple present, use *am / is / are* (see sentence **❶**).

For the simple past, use *was / were* (see sentences **❷** and **❸**).

A Read this profile of Unilever, one of the world's largest companies. Find and circle six examples of the passive.

- Unilever was created in 1930 by a British soap maker and Dutch margarine producer.
- Today 400 brands of home, personal care, and food products are sold by the company.
- Some of the more popular products are Knorr® (soups), Lipton® (tea), and Dove® (soap).
- Lux® soap, which was introduced in 1924, became the first mass-marketed soap in the world.
- Today Knorr® is Unilever's most popular brand. It is sold in over 80 countries.
- The multinational company operates companies and factories on every continent except Antarctica.
- 174,000 people are employed by the company worldwide.
- 160 million times a day, a Unilever product is purchased by someone—somewhere in the world.

B Now rewrite the passive sentences in **A** as active sentences.

1. In 1930, _____ *a British soap maker and Dutch margarine producer created Unilever.* _____

2. Today the company _____.

3. In 1924, a man _____.

4. Today Unilever _____ in over 80 countries.

5. _____ 174,000 people.

6. 160 million times a day, someone in the world _____.

LESSON B

Connecting Ideas with *because, so, although / even though*	
❶ She uses that product **Because** it's the cheapest,	**because** it's the cheapest. she uses that product.
❷ This snack is "100% natural,"	**so** a lot of moms buy it for their kids.
❸ Many people buy that car **Even though / Although** it's expensive,	**even though / although** it's expensive. many people buy that car.

Because, *so*, *although*, and *even though* join two clauses together. A clause has a subject and a verb.

❶ *Because* answers the question *why*. It gives a reason: *Why does she buy that product? (She buys it) because it's the cheapest.*

In conversation, people often give the reason only (*because it's the cheapest*). Don't do this in formal writing. When the clause with *because* comes first, put a comma at the end of the clause.

❷ *So* gives a result: *The snack is "100% natural."* The result: *A lot of moms buy it.*

In writing, use a comma before *so* unless the two clauses are very short.

❸ *Although and Even though* mean the same thing, and they introduce <u>surprising or opposite information</u>: *Many people buy that car <u>even though it's expensive</u>.*

In writing, when the clause with *although / even though* comes first, put a comma at the end of the clause.

A   Complete the sentences with *although / even though*, *because*, or *so*.

1. The phone was on sale, _____*so*_____ many people bought it _____ they didn't need a new phone.

2. A lot of people buy those shoes _____ a famous basketball player wears them.

3. _____ their product is affordable, it doesn't work as well as ours.

4. The new toy was very popular, _____ it sold very quickly.

5. _____ smoking can kill you, many smoking ads show people smiling.

B   Use the connecting words to join the sentences together. Which items can you write in more than one way?

1. That ad is really popular. It has a catchy slogan. (because)

   _____

2. I hate TV commercials. I don't watch much television. (so)

   _____

3. Advertising on TV is very expensive. Companies still do it. (although)

   _____

4. I still bought it. That TV is expensive. (even though)

   _____

5. I decided to try it. My sister liked that shampoo. (so)

   _____

LESSON A

	Describing Symptoms					
	have	**Noun**		**Possessive adjective**	**Noun**	***hurt***
I	have	a headache,	and	my	throat	hurts.
	feel / be	**Adjective**			***can't stop***	***-ing* verb**
I	feel / am	tired,	and	I	can't stop	shivering.

Use *have* + noun, possessive adjective + noun + *hurt*, and *feel / be* + adjective to talk about states and conditions.

Use *can't stop* + *-ing* verb to talk about repeated actions that you have no control over.

Other common vocabulary

have + noun: *I have (a stomachache / an earache / a backache / a toothache / a cut / a sore throat / a fever / a temperature / a cold / the flu).*

possessive adjective + noun + *hurt*: *My (arm / finger / back / leg / stomach) hurts.*
$\qquad\qquad$ *My (legs) hurt.*

feel / be + adjective: *I feel / am (dizzy / nauseous / drowsy / exhausted / faint / weak / sick).*

can't stop + *-ing* verb: *I can't stop (coughing / scratching / sneezing).*

Questions

How do you feel?

Does your head hurt?

What hurts?

Where does it hurt?

A Read the two conversations and complete the sentences. Use the correct form of *be*, *have*, *feel*, *can't stop*, or *hurt*.

Conversation 1

A: What's wrong?

B: I (1.) _____ exhausted. I didn't sleep well last night.

A: (2.) _____ you sick? Maybe you (3.) _____ a cold.

B: No, I'm fine. It's my husband, Fred—he (4.) _____ the flu.

A: I'm sorry to hear that.

B: Yeah, it's pretty bad. He (5.) _____ coughing. It keeps me awake at night. And now my head (6.) _____.

Conversation 2

A: Mom, my stomach (7.) _____.

B: Do you (8.) _____ a fever?

A: No, I don't think so.

B: Do you (9.) _____ nauseous?

A: No, not at all. But you know, I did have potato chips and peanut butter for dinner.

B Write two sentences about each of the pictures on a separate piece of paper. Use the different grammar patterns for describing symptoms.

LESSON B

Reported Speech: Commands and Requests		
	Quoted speech	**Reported speech**
Command	The doctor said, "Get some rest."	The doctor **told** me **to** get some rest.
	The doctor said, "Don't smoke."	The doctor **told** him **not to** smoke.
	Jane's mom said, "Be home at midnight."	Her mom **told** her **to** be home at midnight.
Request	Jon said, "Please turn off your phone."	Jon **asked** me **to** turn off my phone.
	Maria asked, "Can you help me?"	Maria **asked** us **to** help her.
	Chen said, "Please text me later."	Chen **asked** me **to** text him later.

Quoted speech uses a person's exact words: *"Get some rest," said the doctor.*

Reported speech explains what someone else has said: *The doctor **told** me **to** get some rest.*

A **command** is an order: someone tells you what to do.

To report a command, use *tell* + noun / pronoun + (*not*) infinitive (*to* + verb).

If someone makes a **request**, the person is asking you to do something.

To report a request, use *ask* + noun / pronoun + (*not*) infinitive (*to* + verb). Notice how some <u>underlined words</u> change in reported speech.

A Read each quoted command or request. Then complete the sentences in reported speech.

1. "Clean your room!" my mom says every day.

   My mom is always telling me _____.

2. "No texting in class!"

   Our teacher often tells us _____.

3. "Can you loan me some money?"

   Sometimes my friend asks me _____.

4. "Dad, can you drive me to school?"

   Yesterday, I asked my dad _____.

B Read the sentences with quoted speech. Then rewrite each one in reported speech.

1. Coach Jon said to the team, "Don't give up!"

   _____

2. My friends asked me, "Will you help us?"

   _____

3. Anna said to her older sister, "Don't boss me around!"

   _____

4. The librarian said to Mrs. Green, "Please be quiet."

   _____

5. Professor Lewis asked our class, "Please turn in your papers tomorrow."

   _____

6. The parents said to their children, "Don't talk to strangers."

   _____

UNIT 8 THE ACTIVE LIFE

LESSON A

The Present Perfect vs. the Present Perfect Continuous					
	***have / has* + (*not*)**	***been***	**verb + *-ing***		
I	**have(n't)**	**been**	**doing**	much in my spare time.	Use the present perfect continuous for an action that started in the past and continues in the present.
She	**has(n't)**	**been**	**participating**	in the school play.	

Incorrect: ~~**I've been taking** this test three times already~~. Correct: I'**ve taken** this test three times already.	To talk about a repeated action in the past, use the present perfect, not the present perfect continuous.

I've been playing cricket since I was a child. = **I've played** cricket since I was a child.	When you use *for* or *since* to indicate a specific period of time in the past, you can use the present perfect continuous or the present perfect. They have the same meaning.
I've been reading a book on long-distance running. I'm enjoying it. (The action is ongoing.) ≠ **I've read** a book on long-distance running. It was excellent. (The action is completed.)	Some sentences don't indicate a specific time in the past. Use the present perfect continuous for an action that is still happening. Use the present perfect for a completed action. These two sentences have different meanings.
I've been going to the gym a lot lately. Recently **I've been working out** more.	To emphasize that an action has been happening in the recent past up to now, use words like *lately* and *recently* with the present perfect continuous.
Incorrect: ~~**I've been owning** that car for ten years~~. Correct: I'**ve owned** that car for ten years.	As with other continuous tenses, don't use stative verbs (such as *hear*, *like*, and *own*) with the present perfect continuous. Use the present perfect instead.
Incorrect: ~~**I've been taking** this test three times already~~. Correct: I'**ve taken** this test three times already.	To talk about a repeated action in the past, use the present perfect, not the present perfect continuous.

A Tom has started a lot of activities but hasn't finished them. Write five affirmative sentences in the present perfect continuous using the verbs in the box. What is one activity that he hasn't started yet? Write one negative sentence. (Note: The verb *do* is used twice.)

do	eat	study	talk	watch

1. *He's been doing his homework.*
2. ______________________
3. ______________________
4. ______________________
5. ______________________
6. ______________________

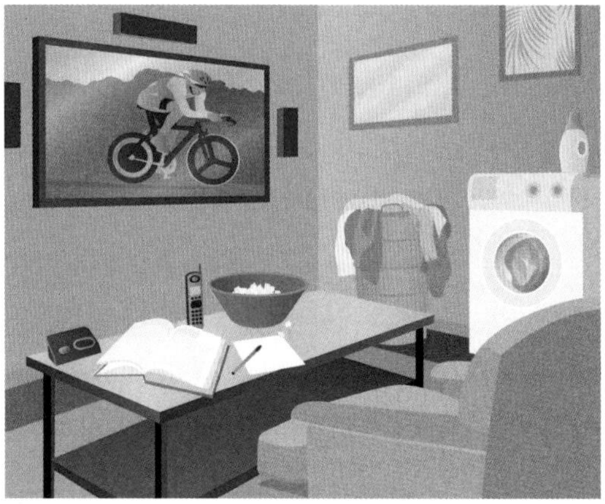

B Circle the correct answer(s) to complete each sentence.

1. I've gotten / I've been getting increasingly active since I joined the judo club.

2. I've belonged / I've been belonging to the club for three months.

3. This is the third time I've taken part / I've been taking part in an extracurricular activity.

4. We've practiced / We've been practicing after school every day since April.

5. My sister has joined / has been joining the photography club.

6. She's taken / She's been taking pictures every day.

LESSON B

Review: The Simple Past vs. the Present Perfect vs. the Present Perfect Continuous		
	Completed past action	**Actions started in the past continuing up to now**
Simple past	❶ I **visited** South Africa <u>in 2010</u>.	
Present perfect	❷ I've **visited** South Africa once.	❸ Fabiola **has skated** for years.
Present perfect continuous		❹ Fabiola **has been skating** for years.

❶ Use the <u>simple past</u> to talk about completed (finished) actions.

❷ You can use the <u>present perfect</u> to talk about past actions if the time they happened is not stated.

In sentence ❶, the speaker says when he was in South Africa: *in 2010.* For this reason, the simple past is used.

In sentence ❷, the speaker has been to South Africa in the past, but he doesn't say when. The present perfect is used.

❸&❹ You can use the <u>present perfect</u> or the <u>present perfect continuous</u> with *for* or *since* to talk about an action that started in the past and continues up to now. Notice that sentences ❸ and ❹ have the same meaning.

Do NOT use the <u>present perfect continuous</u> in the situations below. Use the <u>present perfect</u> instead.

With stative verbs (verbs not used in the continuous like *be*, *have*, *like*, *hate*, *know*, *need*):

~~I've been knowing her for five years.~~   I've **known** her for five years.

To talk about actions that happened a specific number of times:

~~She has been winning the gold medal in the event six times.~~   She **has won** the gold medal in the event six times.

A Read about mountain climber Erik Weihenmayer. Complete the sentences with the verbs in parentheses. Use the present perfect or the present perfect continuous.

Erik Weihenmayer (1. be) _____ blind* since he was 13. He (2. climb) _____ since he was 16, and he's still doing it.

Erik (3. climb) _____ Mount Everest. Also, he (4. reach) _____ the top of the Seven Summits—the seven tallest mountains on the seven continents.

Erik (5. develop) _____ his own climbing system. His partners wear bells on their vests. He follows the sounds of the bells.

Erik (6. think) _____ about his next trip for a long time, but he (7. not choose) _____ a place to go yet.

*blind = unable to see

B Circle the correct verb form to complete each sentence. Sometimes, both answers are possible.

I learned / I've learned how to play dominoes from my grandfather many years ago. He taught / He's been teaching me the game during my summer break from school.

My cousin is 20 years old. He played / He's been playing dominoes since he was seven years old. He's been / He's been being in many dominoes competitions. Last year he got / he's gotten second

(continued)

place in a really big contest. He's always done / He's always been doing well under pressure. I think he'll win first prize this year.

My grandfather has played / has been playing the game for 50 years. He says he's played / he's been playing about 20,000 games, and he doesn't plan to stop.

UNIT **9** SOCIAL ISSUES

LESSON A

Too + Adjective / Adverb; *too much* / *too many* + Noun				
	too	**Adjective / Adverb**	**(Infinitive)**	
You're 17. You're	**too**	young	to vote.	
I can't understand him. He speaks	**too**	quickly.		
	too much* / *too many	**Noun**	**(Infinitive)**	
	Too much	pollution		is bad for your lungs.
Our city has	**too many**	problems	to solve	in one day.

Too means "to a greater degree than is acceptable." It often has a negative meaning.
It comes <u>before</u> adjectives and adverbs.
Use *too much* <u>before</u> noncount nouns.
Use *too many* <u>before</u> plural count nouns.

Adjective / Adverb + *enough*; *enough* + Noun				
	Adjective / Adverb	***enough***	**(Infinitive)**	
I'm 21. I'm	old	**enough**	to vote.	
These are good seats. I can hear	well	**enough**.		
	enough	**Noun**	**(Infinitive)**	
We have	**enough**	water	to get by	for now.
They have	**enough**	police officers		on the street.

Enough means "as much as you need" or "as much as is necessary."
It comes <u>after</u> adjectives and adverbs.
It comes <u>before</u> nouns (count and noncount).

A Complete the reasons on the right with *too*, *too much*, *too many*, or *enough*. Then match the questions with the answers.

1. Why are you so hungry now? ____
2. Why does your stomach hurt? ____
3. Why did you fail the driving test? ____
4. Why didn't you take the driving test? ____
5. Why did you lose the race? ____
6. Why are you running indoors? ____
7. Why did they close the bridge? ____
8. Why didn't you jump off the diving board? ____

a. Because I'm _____ young to drive.
b. Because I ate _____ candy.
c. Because there were _____ people on it.
d. Because it's _____ hot outside.
e. Because I didn't study hard _____.
f. Because I didn't eat _____ breakfast.
g. Because I wasn't brave _____.
h. Because I ran _____ slowly.

B 🔄 Correct the errors with *too* or *enough* below. Check your answers with a partner.

1. I can't button this shirt. It isn't too big.

2. It's not dangerous here. It's enough safe to go out at night by yourself.

3. It's crowded. There are too much people in this little room.

4. These condos are expensive enough to buy. We need more affordable housing.

5. He's only 12 years old. He's old enough to get a driver's license.

LESSON B

Future Real Conditionals	
If clause	**Result clause**
A: What will happen if a woman works? B: If a woman **works**,	(then) a family **will have** more money.
A: What will happen if we don't protect our open spaces? B: If we **don't protect** our open spaces,	(then) future generations **won't have** places to relax.
Result clause	**If clause**
A family **will have** more money	if a woman **works**.

Future real conditionals are used to talk about possibilities or to make predictions. The *if* clause states a possible situation. The result clause says what will or might happen.

The verb in the *if* clause uses the simple present. Don't say: ~~If a woman will work...~~

The verb in the result clause uses a future form. You can also say, for example: *If we don't protect our open spaces, future generations **aren't going to have** places to relax.*

If you aren't certain about the result, you can use *might (not)* or *may (not)* in a result clause:
*If a woman works, a family **may / might have** more money.*

At the start of the result clause, you can use or omit the word *then*. Don't use *then* if the result clause comes first.

The result clause can come first in a sentence with no change in meaning.

In writing, when the *if* clause comes first, put a comma before the result clause.

A Use the simple present or future of the verbs in the box to complete the sentences.

be	~~get~~	make	not pass	not say	not study
educate	have	leave	miss	~~save~~	see

1. You ___'ll save___ money if you ___get___ a roommate.

2. If I _____ all weekend, I _____ the test on Monday.

3. I _____ hello if I _____ him on the street.

4. If you _____ early, you _____ all the fun.

5. It _____ better for the Earth if couples _____ smaller families.

6. If we _____ people, they _____ better decisions.

B Find and correct the mistake in each sentence.

1. If more people will carpool, there will be less traffic on the roads.

2. The school is going to cancel the picnic if it raining tomorrow.

3. If the team won't win tomorrow's game, then they'll be out of the World Cup.

4. You'll make more money in the future if you will go to college.

5. If we destroy the forests, then many animals die.

6. I might visit Italy this summer if I will have enough money.

C For each sentence in **B**, think of one more result and write a conditional sentence. The conditional should be one that follows the sentence in **B**.

1. _If there is less traffic on the roads, people will be happier._ _____

2. _If the school cancels the picnic,_ _____

3. _____

4. _____

5. _____

6. _____

UNIT **10** MONEY

LESSON A

Wish Statements	
Currently I live in the suburbs. I **wish** I <u>lived</u> in the city.	Use the past tense with *wish* to talk about situations that are not true now.
I **wish** (that) I <u>could</u> lend you some money.	Use *could* + base form of the verb with *wish*. *That* is optional in these sentences.
I **wish** (that) I <u>were</u> richer.	Use *were* for all forms of *be* (not *was*).
I can't stick to a budget. I **wish** I could. I don't live in the city. I **wish** I did.	We often shorten *wish* statements in this way.

A Read this joke about Dumb Dave. Complete the sentences with *wish... could* and the verb in parentheses. Why is the character called Dumb Dave?

One day, a genie appeared to Dumb Dave and his three friends. The genie said, "I will give each of you one wish. Don't waste it!"

The first friend said, "(1. fly) _____." Her wish was granted, and she flew away. The second friend said, "(2. live) _____ in a big mansion." He suddenly disappeared, too. The third friend said, "(3. be) _____ a famous actor starring in my own movie." She, too, disappeared.

Dumb Dave looked around and saw that he was alone. Then he said, "I'm lonely. Where have my three friends gone? (4. have) _____ them back here with me now..."

B Imagine that a genie has given you three wishes. What will you wish for? Write three *wish* statements.

1. _____

2. _____

3. _____

LESSON B

Negative Modals		Meaning
Impossibility	You **can't** have the winning lottery ticket. I have it!	Use *can't* to say that something is <u>impossible</u>. It shows surprise or disbelief.
Ability	Sorry, but I **can't** lend you any money. I'm broke.	You can also use *can't* to say you <u>don't have the ability</u> to do something.
Necessity	You **don't have to / don't need to** be rich to travel.	*Don't have to* and *don't need to* mean something <u>isn't necessary</u>. You have a choice.
Advice	You **shouldn't** waste money on expensive cars.	Use *shouldn't* to give advice. It means <u>it's not a good idea</u> to do something.
Strong advice	You**'d better not** lose this ring. It's very valuable.	*Had better not* gives strong advice. It means "I'm <u>warning</u> you not to do something. If you do, there will be a problem."

A Choose the best modal for each sentence.

1. A: Is that John over there driving a Porsche?

   B: It shouldn't / can't be. He doesn't have a driver's license.

2. You'd better not / don't have to lend money to Jack. He won't pay you back.

3. We can't / don't have to study for the test. The teacher canceled it.

4. You shouldn't / can't play the lottery. It's a waste of money.

5. If you've finished your exam, you'd better not / don't need to stay. You can leave.

6. Maria and Kim can't / shouldn't go to the concert. It costs $20, and they only have $10.

B Use the negative form of the modal and the word(s) given to answer speaker A.

1. A: I'm going to spend all my money on a new car.

   B: (had better / squander) _____. Save some!

2. A: My friend Mary wants to borrow some money.

   B: (should / lend) _____. She never pays it back.

3. A: Jane really wants the job, but she doesn't speak Japanese.

   B: (need to / speak) _____ Japanese to get the job.

4. A: We're late for our business class.

   B: (can / be) _____. Class doesn't start until 9:30.

UNIT **11** **HONESTY**

LESSON A

Present Unreal Conditionals	
If clause	**Result clause**
If you **told** the truth,	(then) you **would feel** relieved.
If I **didn't have** a lot of homework,	(then) **I'd go** to the movies.
If I **found** a wallet,	(then) **I'd return** it.
If I **were** a liar,	(then) I **wouldn't have** any friends.
Result clause	**If clause**
You**'d feel relieved**	if you **told** the truth.

Present unreal conditionals are used to talk about imagined or unreal events.

The *if* clause presents an imagined condition. It is not true right now.

The verb in the *if* clause is in the simple past.

With the verb *be*, use *were* for all subjects: *If I <u>were</u> rich, I'd buy a big house.*

In writing, when the *if* clause comes first, put a comma before the result clause.

The result clause presents an imagined result. It can come first or second in the sentence.

The verb in the result clause takes *would* + the base form of the verb.

You can also use *might (not)* (probability) or *could (not)* (ability) in the result clause:

> *If you told them the truth, you <u>might not</u> get into trouble.*
> *If I did something against the law, I <u>could</u> go to jail.*

A Match each situation in **A** to a conditional sentence in **B** and **C**. Use the correct form of the verbs in parentheses.

A	B	C
1. My bicycle is really old.	If I (be) sick,	I (improve / could) them.
2. It's faster to go by subway.	If I ever (lose) it,	I (be / might) late.
3. I feel fine right now.	If I (have) a new one,	I (take / would) some medicine.
4. I love my cell phone.	If I (study) harder,	I (ride / would) it everywhere.
5. My grades aren't very good.	If I (go) by car,	I (buy / would) a new one right away.

1. _My bicycle is really old. If I had a new one, I'd ride it everywhere._

2. _____

3. _____

4. _____

5. _____

B Read the sentences. Circle the answers that are true for you.

1. I'm / I'm not **rich.**

2. I'm / I'm not **a teacher.**

3. I have / don't have **to study English.**

4. I speak / don't speak **English fluently.**

5. I live / don't live **with my parents.**

6. I take / don't take **a bus to school.**

7. I have / don't have **a lot of free time.**

C Now rewrite the sentences in **B** as present unreal conditionals.

1. *If I were rich,* _____
2. _____
3. _____
4. _____
5. _____
6. _____
7. _____

LESSON B

Reported Statements with *say* and *tell*		
Quoted speech	**Reported speech**	
"I **am** an honest person."		he **was** an honest person.
"I **trust** you."		he **trusted** me.
"I **don't believe** you."		he **didn't believe** me.
"I'm **leaving**."		he **was leaving**.
"You **lied** to me."	He **said** (that)	I **had lied** to him.
"I'll **call** you tomorrow."	He **told me** (that)	he **would call** me tomorrow.
"We've never **met**."		we **had** never **met**.
"I **may be** late."		he **might be** late.
"You **must work** harder."		I **had to work** harder.
"You **shouldn't talk** to strangers."		I **shouldn't talk** to strangers.

Quoted speech uses a person's exact words: *"I trust you," said Phil.*

You can report what another person has said using *say* or *tell*.

In reported speech:

The verb tense typically shifts to a past form. Note: *should* usually does not change.

Pronouns change: *"I trust you."* → *Phil said (that) he trusted me.*

The word *that* is optional in the reported sentence.

A Find and correct the error in each sentence.

1. Linda said she will call today, but she didn't keep her word.
2. Denis told to me that he was rich, but that was a lie.
3. Aya says that she had a degree in computer science.
4. Last night, Tim told me he can meet today.
5. Leo said me he spoke French, but he doesn't.

B Gina read Harold's profile on a dating site. She contacted him, and they went on a date. Look at the "real" Harold. Complete what Gina said about him using *say* or *tell*.

(continued)

YOUNG AND HANDSOME GUY LOOKING FOR BEAUTIFUL GIRL

My interests: I work out at the gym every day.

My lifestyle: I don't smoke. I only eat healthy foods. I'm very clean. I drive a sports car.

My talents: I can speak five languages fluently, and I've traveled all over the world.

Let's have dinner and get to know each other; I'll pay for the meal!

1. (say) _He said he was young and handsome_, but he's actually middle-aged and unattractive.

2. (tell) _____, but in fact he rides a bicycle.

3. (say) _____, but actually his house was very messy.

4. (tell) _____, but the truth is he eats a lot of junk food.

5. (say) _____, but actually, he doesn't even have a passport.

6. (tell) _____, but in reality he smokes a lot.

7. (say) _____, but in fact he only speaks English.

8. (tell) _____, but I had to pay for dinner!

UNIT 12 OUR WORLD

LESSON A

Embedded Questions	
To *embed* means to put (something) inside something else. Embedded questions are questions that are included within another question or statement.	
What is a tapir?	Do you know **what a tapir is**?
	I'd like to know **what a tapir is**.
Although we call them embedded <u>questions</u>, they take <u>statement</u> word order.	
How many snow leopards are there?	I wonder **how many snow leopards there are**.
Where do mountain gorillas live?	Do you remember **where mountain gorillas live**?
What is the answer?	I'm not sure **what the answer is**.
These phrases are used to start embedded questions:	
Asking for information	**Saying you don't know something**
Can / Could you tell me…	I don't know / I'd like to know…
Do you know…	I'm not sure…
Do you remember…	I can't remember…
Do you have any idea…	I wonder…
An embedded question can sound softer and less direct than a regular question.	
Excuse me, what time is it?	Excuse me, do you know **what time it is**?

A Unscramble the embedded questions.

1. what / wonder / time / I / opens / it

   _____

2. are / zoo / animals / in / I / what / don't / the / know

   _____

3. I / remember / there / get / how / to / can't / exactly

   _____

4. any / animals / zoo / are / what / the / have / in / you / idea / do

   _____

5. time / it / sure / I'm / opens / what / not

   _____

6. to / do / zoo / you / get / know / to / the / how

   _____

B Now use the sentences in **A** to complete the conversation.

A: Excuse me, _____?

B: _____, but I think you take the #2 train.

A: _____.

B: _____, but it's probably open by now.

A: _____?

B: I'm sorry, but _____.

LESSON B

The Passive with Various Tenses		
	Active	**Passive**
Simple present	Engineers <u>build</u> skyscrapers with a steel frame structure.	Most skyscrapers **are built** with a steel frame structure.
Simple past	The Woolworth Company <u>built</u> a skyscraper in 1913.	One of the first skyscrapers **was built** in 1913.
Present perfect	Engineers <u>have built</u> the world's tallest building in Dubai.	The world's tallest building **has been built** in Dubai.
Present continuous	Engineers <u>are building</u> a lot of tall buildings in Shanghai.	A lot of tall buildings **are being built** in Shanghai.
Simple future	Someday they <u>will build</u> a skyscraper without concrete.	Someday a skyscraper without concrete **will be built**.

A Here are some facts about three important structures. Complete the sentences with the verb and tense in parentheses. Use the passive form of the tense provided.

<u>Itaipu Dam</u>

1. The dam (complete / simple past) _____ in 1991.

2. It (visit / present perfect) _____ by more than nine million people.

<u>Akashi Kaikyo Bridge</u>

3. The record for the longest suspension bridge (hold / simple present) _____ by the Akashi Kaikyo Bridge.

4. The bridge (design / simple past) _____ to be 12,825 feet, but it (make / simple past) _____ even longer after a big earthquake.

<u>Chunnel</u>

5. The first passengers on a Chunnel train were surprised when they (transport / simple past) _____ to the other side in only 20 minutes.

6. In the future, experts predict that even more passengers (carry / simple future) _____ through the Chunnel.

7. While repairs (do / present continuous) _____ to the tunnels, they remain open.

B Think of a famous building, structure, or monument in your city. Answer the questions about it using the passive.

1. Where is it located?

_____

2. When was it built?

_____

3. How many people have visited it?

_____

4. Are any repairs (fixes) being done to it now?

_____

5. What repairs will need to be done in the future?

_____

Answers

Communication page 175, A

1. Singapore **2.** Greenland **3.** Angel Falls **4.** Etna **5.** the Andes **6.** Mammoth Cave **7.** Lake Baikal **8.** the Sahara **9.** Canada